Pearls
of Wisdom

from

RABBI YEHONATAN EYBESHITZ

TORAH GIANT, PREACHER & KABBALIST

Translated by **RABBI YACOV BARBER**

GERBER'S MIRACLE PUBLISHERS

Published by:

Gerber's Miracle Publishers LLC
FORT LAUDERDALE, FL

Copyright © 2021 Gerber's Miracle Publishers LLC

ISBN-13: 978-0-578-85367-3

Copyediting by Carol Killman Rosenberg

Interior production by Gary A. Rosenberg

Cover image used by permission of
"Sinai" Publishing, Tel Aviv, Israel

A portion of the sales of this book
will be donated to Colel Chabad

Contents

PART ONE:
WEEKLY TORAH READINGS

Bereishit (Genesis)

Shemot (Exodus)

Vayikra (Leviticus)

Bamidbar (Numbers)

Devarim (Deuteronomy)

PART TWO:
SHABBAT, THE YOMIM TOVIM, THE BEIT HAMIKDASH, GALUT, AND THE END OF DAYS

Shabbat   118

The 12 Months and the 12 Tribes   129

Rosh Chodesh   131

Rosh Hashanah   133

Yom Kippur: The Ten Days of Repentance   136

Sukkot   139

Chanukah   140

Shabbat Shekalim   143

Zayin Adar   145

Shabbat Zachor   148

Purim   149

Shalosh Regalim (The Three Festivals)   151

Nisan   153

Pesach   154

Shavuot   181

The Messianic Era   231

Publisher's Note

This book is a dream fulfilled for Julie and Richie Gerber. For decades, their wish was to discover a qualified person who would translate the works of Julie's acclaimed ancestor, Rabbi Yehonatan Eybeshitz.

Rabbi Eybeshitz was revered during the early to mid-1700s as a giant Talmudist, master Kabbalist, admired preacher, and author of a voluminous number of books. However, most people today in the Jewish community, with the exception of many in the Orthodox community, do not know about this astounding scholar and his extraordinary ideas.

Rabbi Eybeshitz's books and writings are all in Hebrew, which means most people are not able to read his insightful works. Thirty years ago, Julie and Richie began accumulating Rabbi Yehonatan's books, which sparked a desire to find a capable translator. Their vision was to popularize Rabbi Eybeshitz's "pearls of wisdom."

For Julie, the genesis of revealing Rabbi's Eybeshitz story originated in Poland during the early to mid-1920s. Julie's grandfather (Yosef Ejbszyc), grandmother (Yoheved), their young daughter (Hinde, who later became Julie's mother), and their son (Enrique) traveled from Poland to Cuba. Julie's family spelled their surname *Ejbszyc*, in a more typical Polish way. (Interestingly, there are more than eighty alternative spellings for *Eybeshitz*.)

At that time, life for Jewish people was becoming increasingly difficult, so Julie's grandfather decided to move the family away from all the anti-Semitism taking place in Poland, particularly, in Warsaw where they lived. America was their goal, but at that time, the United States had quotas, so only a limited number of people were permitted to emigrate to America. Avoiding the risk of being trapped in Europe, they set out to travel to a small island in the Caribbean and wait until their quota number was called.

Who would have guessed that once they arrived in Cuba, the Pearl of the Antilles, the Ejbszyc family would be welcomed with open arms? As a matter of fact, many Polish Jews took the same trip and decided to stay in this wonderful island, which offered many opportunities. Growing up an Ejbszyc in Cuba was a wonderful experience for Julie. She was constantly reminded by her mother and other family members that she was descended from "blue blood."

Yosef, now called José, was a man of honor and distinction at his shul in Havana, el Patronato, because of the merit of his great ancestor, Rabbi Eybeshitz. Yoheved became Josefina, known for her delicious Jewish-cooking skills.

A few years after the communist Fidel Castro seized control of the country, the Ejbszyc family fled once again. José and Josefina, their four children with their spouses, as well as all the grandchildren escaped the communist dictatorship and settled in the United States.

Julie—who was the first in the family to escape Cuba as a twelve-year-old—is a direct descendent of Rabbi Yehonatan Eybeshitz through her grandfather, José Ejbszyc.

Julie and Richie married in the early 1970s. Over the years, they had many discussions regarding Julie's famous relative. As they worked on learning about Rabbi Yehonatan's thoughts, teachings, and books, they discovered there was scant information available in English, only biographical writings. Though they had amassed quite a large collection of books authored by Rabbi Yehonatan, they could not read Hebrew. For them, the dream of translating Rabbi Yehonatan's words into English became a passion. Over the years, they searched for that one special individual who would be able to fulfill their dream.

Miracles happen when you least expect them. Several years ago, Julie and Richie had the good fortune to meet Rabbi Efraim Duchman, a director of Colel Chabad, an outstanding organization that assists the needy in Israel. When speaking to Rabbi Duchman, Richie told him about his life's quest to find a translator for Rabbi Eybeshitz's words. And, to his surprise, Rabbi Duchman did not hesitate. He immediately recommended his father-in-law, Rabbi Yacov Barber. Richie and Julie would soon discover Rabbi Barber's elevated knowledge of Rabbi Yehonatan Eybeshitz and tremendous experience as a writer.

The Gerbers gratefully thank Rabbi Efraim Duchman for connecting them to Rabbi Yacov Barber, who has made this book possible. They owe a huge debt of gratitude to Rabbi Efraim Duchman for helping them realize their dream.

When they met, the Gerbers had instant chemistry with Rabbi Barber, who was very familiar with the words of Julie's ancestor and easily developed a vision for a book that answered all their prayers. In the pages to follow, you will be reading the words of Rabbi Yehonatan as translated by Rabbi Yacov Barber.

Words cannot express the Gerbers' gratitude to Rabbi Barber for bringing their dream into reality. He has expertly brought the words of Julie's ancestor to all of our eyes.

Preface

THIS IS THE THIRD BOOK I HAVE WRITTEN. Each book was very different in style. The first was *Generation to Generation*, which is a compilation of sources on the Haggadah. The second was *Wit and Wisdom*, which contains short sermons on the weekly Torah reading. This book is a translation of some of the writings of Rabbi Yehonatan Eybeshitz. Rabbi Yehonatan was known as one of the greatest rabbis of his era. He had thousands of students and wrote some of the most important works on Jewish law and Jewish thought.

I would like to thank my son-in-law Rabbi Ephraim Duchman for being the *shadchan* who introduced me to Richie and Julie Gerber. Julie is a direct descendant of Rabbi Yehonatan Eybeshitz. Julie and Richie are very proud of their lineage, and they wanted to make some of Rabbi Yehonatan's writings available to the English-speaking public. Their passion and enthusiasm to see this work reach its fruition was truly contagious. I would like to thank them sincerely for entrusting me with this monumental work.

A very special thank-you to the highly professional team at The Book Couple, Carol Killman Rosenberg for her editing; it took my work to a new level. And to Gary Rosenberg, for designing and producing this book. Its design and layout are testament to his great ability and talent.

I would like to dedicate this book in the memory of beloved family members who have passed away. While they are no longer present in this physical world, their memory and their shining example live on in their children, grandchildren, and great grandchildren.

My late wife, Rivkie, who passed away on 19 Adar 2 5775. Rivkie was a respected rebbetzin and a devoted teacher. Her warmth and friendliness, humor and vibrancy, authenticity and compassion touched the lives of all who crossed her path. However, her greatest achievement was the way she raised our six beautiful children. Baruch Hashem, many of them are married and have established their own homes. The greatest nachas Rivkie a"h and I have is seeing the way they are raising their children, in the manner they saw in our home and the homes of their grandparents.

My late father, Reb Meir Barber, who passed away on the 18 Elul 5779. He was one of the pillars of the Sydney *frum* community. My father was a Holocaust survivor; he spent most of the war years with his family in Siberia. He was a child when the war broke out and never really had the opportunity to study in a yeshivah. After the war, he ended up in Bergen-Belsen. He attended a yeshivah that had been established in what was once the infamous concentration camp. He eventually made his way to Sydney, Australia, and in his small suitcase he brought with him one of our family's great treasures. He brought his Gemorah with him. On the first page, it says his name and the name of the yeshivah, *Sheirit Hapleito* Bergen-Belsen. Perhaps this encapsulates the secret of Jewish survival. The recognition of the inseparable bond between the Torah and the Jewish people. It speaks of the strength of the Jewish people that even in our darkest hours we continue to learn and teach G-d's Torah. That Gemorah continues to inspire his children, grandchildren, and great grandchildren to this very day.

My late father-in-law, Rabbi Asher Halevi Heber, who passed away on 8 Nisan 5780. He merited that the Lubavitcher Rebbe and Rebbetzin were the *kevaterin* at his bris in prewar Paris. For over forty years, he was a beloved teacher in Manhattan Jewish Day School. It was astounding to hear and read the accolades his students shared with the family after his untimely passing. Many had been in his class more than thirty years earlier, and they were still able to recall so much of what he had taught them and how he inspired them to lead Torah-observant lives coupled with a great thirst for the study of Torah.

My beloved uncle and aunt, Reb Shabsi and Rebecca Kornwasser. Reb Shabsi, who passed away on 2 Adar 5772, came from an illustrious family of Radomsk Chasidim. He was an everlasting link of the Chasidic world of prewar Poland and the Jewish world I grew up in in Australia. His stories of Chasidic life in Sosnowiec and his heroic self-sacrifice for Torah and mitzvot during the Holocaust inspire me to this very day.

Auntie Becca, as she was affectionately known, passed away on 21 Shvat 5779. She was beloved by everyone; she was imbued with great *simchat hachayim* (love of life), which she shared with all who knew her. One could say she lived to give. She had a heart of gold and only saw the good in people.

To my dear mother, Esther Barber, and my dear *shviger*, Nechama Heber. May you both find a level of solace in seeing the beautiful generations you are both the proud matriarchs of. May Hashem bless you both with many years of good health and be *zoche* to greet *Moshiach Tzidkeiynu b'karov mamosh.*

—Rabbi Yacov Barber

18 Elul 5780
Marking the first yahrzeit of my father,
   Reb Meir Barber a"h

Introduction

WITHOUT DOUBT, ONE OF THE GREATEST TORAH SCHOLARS of the last 300 years was Rabbi Yehonatan Eybeshitz—a Rav, Rosh Yeshivah, and Darshan. A prolific writer covering the vast gamut of Torah scholarship, he was among the leading Halachic deciders of his generation. His scholarly works are studied to this very day in yeshivot and kollelim throughout the world. Any rabbi giving a halachic ruling will seek out Rabbi Yehonatan's writings on the topic. His seforim—especially those that deal with halachic topics—are complex and demand a great deal of prior knowledge.

Rabbi Yehonatan wrote extensively on the weekly Torah reading and the Yomim Tovim (festivals). His insights on the Torah, as well as his approach to his thoughts on the Yomim Tovim, are diverse in style and content. Rabbi Yehonatan was a darshan, and his writings—especially his work the *Yaaroth Devash*—reflect this.

It is important to convey that this sefer does not fall under the category of light reading. Rather, each thought should be read a number of times (even if one understands the idea after the first reading) to fully appreciate the various subtleties being conveyed.

I have attempted to give you a taste of the prolific writings of Rabbi Yehonatan and the many and varied styles of interpretation. The thoughts on the weekly Torah reading are mainly gleaned from the Tiferet Yehonatan unless otherwise stated. Any ambiguity in understanding or mistakes in the ideas presented lie squarely on my shoulders. I pray and hope that I have accurately conveyed Rabbi Yehonatan's thoughts and ideas, and you will be excited by studying them as I was in sharing them.

—Rabbi Yacov Barber

The Life of
Rabbi Yehonatan Eybeshitz

RABBI YEHONATAN EYBESHITZ WAS ONE OF THE GREATEST rabbis of the eighteenth century. His writings cover all areas of Jewish Learning, including the Talmud, the Shulchan Aruch (the Code of Jewish Law), homiletics, and Kabbalah. Even as a child, he was renowned as one of the rare geniuses of his time. He served as rabbi of various communities for more than fifty years. He founded and led yeshivot for most of his life. His students became the leading rabbis and teachers of the next generation.

Rabbi Yehonatan was born in Pintshov, Poland, on the 6th of Cheshvan, 1696,[1] to parents Rabbi Nosson Nota and Shaindel Tzuntz. His mother passed away while he was still a young boy. When Yehonatan was eleven years old, his father was appointed as Av Beth Din (head) of the Rabbinical Court in the city of Eybeschutz (Morovia) and the head of the yeshivah, which the young Yehonatan attended. Tragically, a year later, Yehonatan's father passed away. Rabbi Yehonatan then took on the family name Eybeschutz for the city in which he had lived most of his young life.

The rabbis of Eybeschutz felt that Rabbi Yehonatan should relocate to the yeshivah of Rabbi Meir Eisenstadt. He became a beloved

---

1. A number of sources have Rabbi Yehonatan born in 1690 or 1692. In the sefer Toldot Gedolei Hador, it is written that Rabbi Yehonatan was born in 1696. The reason 1696 appears to be more accurate is based on the following: It seems everyone agrees that he married in 1710. If he was born 1690, he would have been 20 years old when he married. During that period, men of his stature would marry at age 14 or 15, which is more consistent with the opinion that he was born in 1696.

student of the yeshivah. A year later, Rabbi Meir Eisenstadt left the yeshivah and returned to Poland. As a result, Rabbi Yehonatan relocated to the yeshivah of his uncle Rabbi Eliezer Segal in the city of Holishvaya. Rabbi Yehonatan excelled in his learning, and many sought him as a suitable husband for their daughters.

In 1710, at the age of fourteen, Rabbi Yehonatan married Elkeli, the daughter of Rabbi Yitzchak Shapiro. The young newlywed couple moved to Rabbi Yitzchak's hometown of Bemusela. Rabbi Yitzchak was the head of the yeshivah in Bemusela. A year later, when Rabbi Yehonatan was only fifteen years old, Rabbi Yitzchak appointed him as the head of the yeshivah. That same year, in 1711, Rabbi Yehonatan relocated to the city of Prague and learned under his father-in-law's father, Rabbi Aharon Yechiel Michel Shapiro. He also studied under his father-in-law's grandfather, Rabbi Benyamin Volf, who was Av Beth Din and the rabbi of the city. Rabbi Yehonatan also studied under the Korban Netanel.

In 1713, an epidemic broke out in Prague, and as a result, Rabbi Yehonatan, together with his wife and children, moved to Hamburg where his mother-in-law's father, Rabbi Mordechai Cohen, lived. A year later, in 1714, the *darshan* (preacher) of Prague passed away, and the rabbis of Prague requested that Rabbi Yehonatan accept the position of darshan. Rabbi Yehonatan's speeches electrified his audiences, and synagogues were filled whenever he spoke. Sometimes he would speak for seven or eight hours straight.

A mere few months after being appointed darshan, Rabbi Yehonatan was appointed the Rosh Yeshivah (head rabbi) of the yeshivah of Prague. During the years he headed the yeshivah, Rabbi Yehonatan's fame spread throughout the Jewish world. Questions to him were sent from far and near. His fame also spread among the gentile world. He debated many leaders of the church on various topics. As a result of his close relationship with the heads of the church, Rabbi Yehonatan received permission to print the Talmud.

Twenty-three years after being appointed the darshan of Prague, the Av Beth Din Rabbi Dovid Oppenheim passed away. As a result, Rabbi Yehonatan was appointed Av Beth Din. Rabbi Yehonatan now held three positions in Prague: the Rosh Yeshivah, the darshan, and the Av Beth Din.

After spending twenty-eight years in Prague, Rabbi Yehonatan and his family moved to Metz, France. In Metz, Rabbi Yehonatan built a yeshivah that flourished. Then, in 1750, the communities of Altona, Hamburg, and Wansbeck in Germany appointed him their chief rabbi. Rabbi Yehonatan was keen to relocate there because he was eager to have his writings printed, and Metz did not have a publishing house like these three cities did.

Soon after arriving at his new rabbinical post, Rabbi Yehonatan became embroiled in a dispute with Rabbi Ya'akov Emden, a well-known German rabbi, that engulfed much of the Jewish world. At that time, a terrible plague was sweeping through the Jewish people; women were dying during childbirth. Because Rabbi Yehonatan was known as a great kabbalist, many women would go to him for a blessing to protect them during childbirth, and he would write amulets for them. Meanwhile, a number of years prior, Shabtai Zvi, a rabbi from Smyrna, claimed to be the messiah, and many Jewish people had accepted him as such. However, it soon became evident that Shabtai Zvi was a fraud; nonetheless, he had created havoc among the Jewish people. Those who were opposed to Rabbi Yehonatan took some of the amulets he had made to Rabbi Ya'akov Emden and claimed that Rabbi Yehonatan was a secret follower of Shabtai Zvi, which was completely false. The dispute between the rabbis lasted until 1756, when it finally became evident that the claims had been fabricated.

In 1755, Rabbi Yehonatan's beloved wife passed away. Then, on the 21st of Elul in 1764, at the age of sixty-eight, Rabbi Yehonatan passed away. Rabbi Yehonatan and his wife were blessed with six sons (Reb Yehudah Leib, Reb Yitzchak, HaRav Nosson Nota, Reb Morde-chai, Reb Yechiel Michel, and Reb Binyamin Zev), and three daughters (Rivkah, Hitzel, and Nisel).

Rabbi Yehonatan's Writings

Rabbi Yehonatan left behind many writings on all sections of the Torah. His main works on Halacha (Jewish law) are:

The Urim Vetumim on Shulchan Aruch Choshen Mishpat (Monetary Law)

Kereisi Upleisi on Shulchan Aruch Yore De'ah (Dietary Law)

He also wrote a book on *derash* (homiletics) called the *Yaaroth Devash*.

He wrote more than thirty seforim.

PART ONE

Weekly Torah Readings

Bereishit

Note: Certain words can be written with or without the letter vov.

> *And God said, "Let there be luminaries in the expanse of the heavens, to separate between the day and between the night, and they shall be for signs and for appointed seasons and for days and years. And they shall be for luminaries in the expanse of the heavens to shed light upon the earth,"*
> *and so it was.* (Bereishit 1:14–15)

The word *luminaries* appears twice in the foregoing verses. The first time it is written without the letter *vov*, and the second time it is written with the letter *vov*. Why the change?

The moon has no independent light; it reflects the light of the sun. The first time *luminaries* is written, the verse is referring to the heavens, and in heaven, it is known that the moon has no independent light. Therefore, the world *luminaries* is written without the *vov* to indicate that something is lacking—this being the moon having no light of its own.

The second time *luminaries* is written, it is referring to the sun and the moon shedding light upon the earth. By simply looking at the moon, a person on earth would come to the conclusion that the moon has its own source of light. Therefore, the word *luminaries* is written with a *vov*.

> *And God said, "Let there be luminaries in the expanse of the heavens, to separate between the day and between the night, and they shall be for signs and for appointed seasons and for days and years. And they shall be for luminaries in the expanse of the heavens to shed light upon the earth, and so it was.* (Bereishit 1:14–15)

This verse seems to be somewhat repetitive. Also, what is the distinction between the phrase "to separate between the day and between the night" and the phrase "to shed light upon the earth"?

The first verse "to separate between day and night" is referring to heaven. As in heaven, there is no need for the sun and the moon to shine their light—as in heaven, there is always light. The sun and the moon's function in heaven is to *separate between day and night*. As the Midrash explains, Moshe knew it was night when he saw the sun to the west. He knew when it was day when he saw the sun to the east.

The second verse "to shed light upon the earth" is referring to earth. On earth, there isn't any light; we need the sun and moon to *shed light upon the earth*.

> *Therefore a man shall forsake his father and mother*
> *and cleave to his wife, and they shall become one flesh*
> (Bereishit 2:24)

What is the connection between "a man shall forsake his father and mother" and the next phrase "and cleave to his wife and they shall become one flesh"?

Many believe there are two partners in the birth of a child: the father and the mother. Judaism believes there are three partners: the father, the mother, and God. The father and mother contribute the physical makeup of the child, while God contributes the soul. A couple, when they marry, are from two sets of parents. They may also come from two different parts of the world from two totally different backgrounds and upbringings. What is surprising is how much the couple has in common, and they seem to be copies of one another. The reason this is so is because the true essence of a person is their soul. Each individual possesses a half a soul, and when they marry their *bashert* (soul mate), the two half souls unite, and the couple now forms a single soul. That is why the couple has so much in common; together, they are one soul.

The connection between the two parts of the verse can be understood thus: "Therefore a man shall forsake his father and mother" means a person should *forsake* the thought that he is the sole product of *his father and mother*; rather, there is a third partner—God. God contributes the two half souls, and when a couple marries, their two half souls unite as one. This being the case, it is feasible for the husband to "cleave to his wife and they shall become one flesh."

Noach

And Noach found favor in the eyes of God. (Bereishit 6:8)

These are the descendants of Noach (Bereishit 6:9)

What is the connection between these two verses?

There were ten generations between Adam and Noach and ten generations between Noach and Abraham. The rabbis teach us that God delays His anger for ten generations. Mankind started to sin in the times of Adam; therefore, the generation of Noach needed to be punished. Once permission has been given to the spiritual forces of destruction, the forces don't distinguish between the righteous and the wicked, and Noach and his family should have perished in the flood as well. The reason they didn't was because *Noach found favor in the eyes of God.* Why did he find favor? Because of *the descendants of Noach.* Who was Noach's descendant? Abraham.

It was in the merit of Abraham that Noach was saved.

This understanding explains the connection between these two verses. Based on this understanding, we can offer a unique interpretation of a verse in Mishlei (Proverbs) 12:7. The verse reads:

"The wicked will be overthrown."

The Hebrew word for *wicked* is spelled *resh, shin, ayin, yud, mem.* The first three letters—*resh, shin, ayin*—can be rearranged to read *ayin, shin, resh,* which spells the word *eser,* which means *ten.* The last two letters—*yud, mem*—spell the word *yam,* which means *sea.* By rearranging the letters of the word *wicked,* the verse "The wicked will be overthrown" can be understood to mean, after ten generations (from Adam until the times of Noach), the wicked will be thrown into the sea (the flood).

These are the descendants of Noach (Bereishit 6:9)

The opening word of this week's Torah reading—*These*—can be understood in a negative light. Noach was blessed with three sons. He was, however, unsuccessful at convincing any other person in recognizing God. *These* (his biological children) embraced God, but no other—unlike Abraham who converted many idol worshippers to abandon their belief, embrace monotheism, and believe in the God of Abraham.

Why then did Noach and his family merit being saved from the flood that destroyed the world? The verse continues:

Noach walked with God (Bereishit 6:9)

Noach and his family accepted and embraced the God of Israel.

This contrast between Abraham and Noach answers a problematic statement found in the writing of Rambam. Rambam writes that no human being recognized God until Abraham. Clearly, Noach recognized God: he built the ark, which took him 120 years.

Rambam did not mean that Abraham was the first human being to recognize God. What he was really saying was that Abraham was the first person to influence others in recognizing God, which is something Noach was unable to do.

And take for yourself food that is eaten and gather it in to you,
and it shall be for you and for them to eat (Bereishit 6:21)

God performed a miracle: Though the ark was not physically large enough to contain the whole animal kingdom, it was able to do so. We must say a similar thing concerning food. How was the ark large enough to contain enough food to feed all the animals for close to a year? Especially considering it was just prior to Noach and his family entering the ark that he was told how many of each species he should take. Therefore, the verse says, "take for yourself food." You are responsible to ensure you and your family have enough food for a year. God will perform a miracle: "it shall be for you and for them to eat"—what you had prepared for yourself will now be sufficient for all the animals as well.

And the Lord said to Himself, "I will no longer curse the earth because of man." (Bereishit 8:21)

Note: The flood took place in 2105 BCE. In 1765 BCE, mankind built the Tower of Babel. Mankind was punished for building the tower.

"The Lord said to Himself"—why did God only tell Himself that he would no longer bring another flood to destroy the world? Why did the generation of the Tower of Babel attempt to rebel against God? They knew how God had brought a flood and wiped out all of humanity. What were they trying to accomplish by building the tower? Did they really believe they could build a tower that could reach God?

God did not want to inform mankind that He would never bring another flood in order that mankind should be afraid and, as a result, they wouldn't sin. Therefore, God said to *Himself*, "I will no longer curse the earth."

The people at the time of the Tower of Babel knew they were sinners, and they were worried that God may bring another flood and destroy the world. They therefore built the tower to save themselves. They felt a tower would save them for the following reasons:

1. Rain comes from the clouds. They thought, *If we can build a tower that will be higher than the clouds, even if God will bring a flood, we will be saved since we will be higher than the clouds.*

2. The people of the time were aware of the laws of gravity. They also were aware that once a person goes beyond the earth's atmosphere, there will no longer be the pull of gravity to bring them back to earth.

They said let us build a tower that will reach beyond the atmosphere. Then we will build a spaceship that will float in the heavens, and we will take the spaceship to the moon, and we will inhabit the moon. They were under the impression that mankind could live on the moon.

The people knew how to build ships, as we see Noach was able to build one. Also, the people knew that the earth was divided into two great land masses—one being Asia, Africa, and Europe and the other being America. If they didn't know how to build ships, how were they able, at that time, to travel to the area that came to be known as America? We must say there were people living in America at the time of the flood because otherwise there would have been no need to destroy it.

The flood did not cover the Land of Israel; it was therefore referred to as *Tehorah* (a pure land). If the flood did not cover America, it should have been referred to as *Tehorah*, and there is no mention of this in respect to America.

Lech Lecha

Note: The Amidah, part of the daily service, begins with the blessing, "Blessed are you, God, our God and the God of our fathers. The God of Abraham, the God of Yitzchak, and the God of Ya'akov."

And I will make you into a great nation, and I will bless you,
and I will make your name great, and you shall be a blessing.
(Bereishit 12:2)

The Talmud (Pesachim 117b) explains the verse in the following manner: "And I will make you into a great nation," and therefore, we begin the Amidah by saying the God of Abraham; "and I will bless you," and therefore, we say the God of Yitzchak; "and I will make your name great," and therefore, we say the God of Ya'akov. The Talmud does not explain the final phrase of the verse "and you shall be a blessing."

Perhaps we can explain it in the following manner: In the Messianic era, God will extend a cup of wine to Abraham and ask him to make the blessing. Abraham will decline, and his rationale for declining will be because he had a son, Yishmael, who was not righteous. God will then ask Yitzchak to make the blessing, and he too will refuse on the grounds that he had a son, Esau, who was wicked. God then asks Ya'akov, who will refuse because he married two sisters.

Finally, God asks King David to make the blessing. King David agrees, as it is alluded to in Tehillim (Psalms) 116:13, where King David says:

I shall lift up a cup of salvations and I shall call out in the
name of the Lord.

Therefore, when the verse says, "you shall be a blessing," this is referring to King David, who will make the blessing on the cup of wine in the Messianic era.

Please say that you are my sister. (Bereishit 12:13)

Note: Abraham and Sarah left Israel due to the famine in the land and made their way to Egypt. Frightened the Egyptians would kill him if they discovered he was the husband of Sarah, Abraham requested that Sarah, when asked, say she was his sister.

While it is true Abraham was scared for his life and felt that if the Egyptians believed they were brother and sister, his life would be spared. He was asking Sarah to lie. Is such behavior acceptable?

When they were living in Israel, our forefathers had the status of Jewish people. When they traveled outside Israel, they had the status of a Noahite. According to the Noahite law, if a married couple seeks a divorce, the husband only needs to tell his wife, "You are no longer my wife." And the wife needs to respond, "You are no longer my husband." Therefore, when Abraham said to Sarah, "Say you are my sister," that was tantamount to divorcing her.

As a result, there was no underhanded action on the part of Abraham. Abraham and Sarah were in Egypt; they were bound by Noahite law. By each saying, "We are brother and sister," they were divorced.

Vayeira

And God appeared to him (Abraham) at the plains of Mamre.
(Bereishit 18:1)

Abraham was circumcised at age ninety-nine. On the third day after his circumcision, God went to visit him. The question is asked why the Torah mentions that the visit took place in the plains that belonged to Mamre. The answer given: It was Mamre who encouraged Abraham to have the circumcision.

It seems hard to imagine that, if God had instructed Abraham to have a circumcision, he would need convincing from Mamre to follow through with God's instruction. Abraham, of course, did not need to be convinced; rather, Mamre encouraged him to circumcise himself during the day and not at night. Why was it important for Abraham to circumcise himself during the day and not at night?

Abraham dedicated his life to encourage humanity to renounce idol worship and embrace monotheism. It is interesting to note that no individual or group of people attempted to kill Abraham. Perhaps one could say that Abraham was a mighty warrior, and people were frightened. However, when Abraham was weak after being circumcised, this would be an opportune time for him to be attacked.

If Abraham would have had the circumcision at night, the nations may have said he did it at night when no one could see or discover what he did because he was frightened. Therefore, Mamre encouraged him to have it as public as possible, and no one would attack him, thereby increasing the miracle.

Therefore, God appeared to Abraham in the plains of Mamre in a most public manner.

And God appeared to him (Abraham) at the plains of Mamre.
(Bereishit 18:1)

The Midrash says that God visited Abraham on the third day after his circumcision to see how he was feeling. The commentaries ask why God waited three days to visit Abraham when it is known that the day of circumcision is the most painful.

Rashi is of the opinion that Abraham was circumcised on the first day of Pesach (Passover). The Tosafists are of the opinion that he was circumcised on Yom Kippur (Day of Atonement). The Talmud (Shabbat 12a) states that you cannot visit the sick on Shabbat or Yom Tov. The Talmud (Sotah 14a) states that we need to emulate God. Just as God visits the sick, we too should visit the sick.

If God visited Abraham on Yom Tov, then we too should be able to visit the sick on Yom Tov, which would be contrary to the Talmud's statement in Shabbat 12a. Therefore, the Midrash informs us that God did not visit Abraham on the day of circumcision; rather, he visited Abraham on the third day after his circumcision, as that day was not a Yom Tov.

Chayei Sarah

Abraham came to eulogize Sarah and he cried. (Bereishit 23:2)

In this week's Torah reading, Sarah passes away. It is interesting to note that the verse tells us that Abraham first eulogizes Sarah, and then he cries. Normally, a person cries and then says a eulogy. The Talmud states that the first three days after a person passes away are considered days of crying and after the days of crying begin the days of eulogies.

Why, by Abraham, does it first mention eulogy and *then* crying? The verse began by saying, "Abraham came." The question is posed: Where was Abraham coming from? One of the answers given is that he was coming from the funeral of his father, Terach.

If Abraham was crying when he arrived to bury Sarah, one couldn't be sure why he was crying: Was it because he had lost his father or because he had lost his wife?

Therefore, the verse begins by saying Abraham initially gave a eulogy in memory of his wife and then he began to cry, clearly indicating that he was now crying for the passing of Sarah and not for the passing of his father, Terach.

And Abraham was old, advanced in days (Bereishit 24:1)

On this verse, the Midrash quotes a verse in Tehillim (Psalms) 90:10:

The days of our years because of them are seventy years.

This seems to imply that Abraham was seventy years old at the time, when in fact he was one hundred and forty years old. Abraham was a hundred years old when Yitzchak was born. Yitzchak was forty years old when he married—and this verse was said when Abraham's servant, Eliezer, went to find a wife for Yitzchak.

When Abraham was seventy years old, God established the covenant with him. At the time of the covenant, we consider Abraham as if he was a newborn person. In our verse, Abraham is one hundred forty years old; if we remove the seventy years prior to the covenant, Abraham is in fact seventy years old. The Midrash that said, "the days of our lives because of them are seventy years" is referring to Abraham after removing the seventy years prior to the covenant.

Toldot

The children struggled inside her. She said, "If so why did I need this," and she went to seek out God. God said to her, "Two esteemed individuals are in your womb. Two kingdoms will sprout from your innards. One kingdom will become mightier than the other kingdom. The older will serve the younger."
(Bereishit 25:22–23)

Yitzchak and Rivkah had been married for twenty years, and they had not been blessed with children. Rivkah fell pregnant, and she experienced something very troubling. When she would pass a house of worship or a house of God, she felt as if the fetus was trying to leave her womb. When she walked past a house of idol worship, she also felt as if the fetus was trying to leave her womb.

God informed her, "Two esteemed individuals are in your womb." She initially thought she was carrying one child; God informed her that she was carrying twins.

Note: There are many interpretations of these verses. Presented are some of the thoughts mentioned in the Tiferet Yehonatan:

1. Rivkah had not been able to fall pregnant for twenty years. She saw herself becoming pregnant as a miracle from God. She therefore couldn't understand that if God had performed a miracle, why would the fetus be drawn to a place of idol worship? God informed her that she was carrying twins: Ya'akov and Esau. And while Esau was wicked, many of his descendants would convert to Judaism. While Esau was evil, from the evil would come goodness. When God informs her, "One kingdom will become mightier than the other kingdom," this is alluding to the idea that Ya'akov would merit and receive great strength due to the suffering and exile at the hands of Esau.

2. Rivkah initially thought she was carrying one child, and this one

child was drawn to serve God and to serve idols. Rivkah thought that the child would mistakenly believe that a person is permitted to serve God and at the same time serve idols, as God had vested the idols with independent power and authority. Rivkah therefore cried out, "Why do I need this?" The Hebrew word Rivkah used for the word *I* is *anochi*. The more common word normally used for *I* is *ani*. By specifically using the word *anochi*, Rivkah was alluding to the first commandment of the ten commandments. The first commandment begins with God saying, "I am the lord your God." The Hebrew word God uses for *I* is *anochi*, the same word Rivkah used. Rivkah was asking, "How can I have a child who will not keep the first and second commandment?" The first the belief in one God and the second to not believe in other gods? Therefore, God informed her, "You are carrying two children."

3. Rivkah asked God, "Why am I carrying two children—a righteous child and a wicked child—why can't each child be born to a different mother?" God responded, "The reason you are carrying twins is in order that sometimes one nation will overpower the other and vice versa, and it will be dependent on the righteousness of each particular generation."

4. In those times, a women usually gave birth in the seventh month and not during the ninth month. Giving birth in the seventh month is less painful than during the ninth month as the fetus is smaller. Rivkah was asking, "Why am I not giving birth like most women during the seventh month?" God tells her, "The older will serve the younger"—therefore, each fetus wants to be born second so that the child born first will serve the child born second.

She said, "If so why did I need this," and she went to seek out God. (Bereishit 25:22)

Rivkah went to seek out God. Rashi explains that she went to the house of study of Shem, the son of Noach. The question posed is:

Why didn't she seek the advice of Abraham, who was still alive at the time? The rabbis tell us that Abraham passed away prior to when he was supposed to so that he wouldn't see his grandson Esau grow into a wicked person.

If Rivkah would have gone to see Abraham and she would have told him what she was experiencing when she passed a house of idol worship, he would have realized that his grandson was going to be wicked. Therefore, things were put in place for Rivkah to go to Shem rather than to Abraham.

Yitzchak loved Esau because (he provided) his mouth with game. (Bereishit 25:28)

Rashi explains that Esau would entrap Yitzchak and deceive him with words. Esau would ask his father, "How does one give tithe from salt and how does one give tithe from grain?" Why did Esau specifically ask questions about giving tithe?

Esau did not believe that God rewards people in the world to come. However, he did believe that God rewards people for certain commandments in this world. One of the commandments for which God rewards people in this world is the giving of tithe. Therefore, Esau specifically asked his father about the obligations involving tithe.

Vayetzei

While he was still talking with them, Rachel came with her father's sheep for she was a shepherdess. (Bereishit 29:9)

In this week's Torah reading, Ya'akov marries Leah and Rachel. Laban, their father, wanted Leah (his older daughter) to marry Esau (the older brother), while Rachel (his younger daughter) should marry Ya'akov (the younger brother).

Laban knew that Esau was a man of the field; he therefore wanted Leah to be involved in the running of the house so the couple would complement each other. Ya'akov was a person who spent most of his time in the tent immersed in prayer and study. Laban therefore wanted Rachel to be a shepherdess to create a balance with Ya'akov. Therefore, the Torah is informing us "she was a shepherdess," while Leah was not a shepherdess.

And Laban said to Ya'akov, "Because you are my family, should you work for nothing? Tell me what your wages should be." (Bereishit 29:15)

When Rivkah was pregnant with Ya'akov and Esau, God said there would be times when the younger would serve the older and the older would serve the younger.

This is what Laban was alluding to when he said, "Because you are my family, should you work for nothing?" In other words, "If I was Esau, your brother, then perhaps you should work for me for nothing because you would be my slave. However, I am not Esau; therefore, tell me what your wages should be."

Vayishlach

And Jacob was left alone, and a man wrestled with him until the break of dawn. When he saw that he could not prevail against him, he touched the socket of his hip, and the socket of Jacob's hip became dislocated as he wrestled with him. And he (the angel) said, "Let me go, for dawn is breaking," but he (Ya'akov) said, "I will not let you go unless you have blessed me." So he said to him, "What is your name?" and he said, "Ya'akov." And he said, "Your name shall no longer be called Ya'akov, but Israel, because you have commanding power with [an angel of] God and with men, and you have prevailed." (Bereishit 32:25–29)

In this week's Torah reading, Ya'akov battled with the angel the whole night. Ya'akov asked the angel to bless him, and the angel said, "Your name shall no longer be called Jacob, but Israel." Till that point, Ya'akov had to get what was rightfully his in a deceitful manner such as the right to be considered the firstborn and the blessings from his father Yitzchak. The angel told Ya'akov from now on you will be called Yisrael (Israel). The last two letters of Ya'akov's new name are *aleph* and *lamed*—a name of God. This name represents strength. With his new name Yisrael (Israel), Ya'akov would take whatever he wants with great strength.

Angels don't have a set name. Their names are dependent on what task God has instructed them in fulfilling. Therefore, Ya'akov asked the angel, "What is your name?" Ya'akov was asking about the main purpose of their encounter: Was it to do battle with him or was the main purpose to bless him with a new name? To which the angel responded, "I have two names because I had to fulfill two distinct tasks."

And Ya'akov came safely to the city of Shechem
(Bereishit 33:18)

Note: A Cohen who has a physical defect cannot serve in the temple.

Rashi points out that Ya'akov, at that point, was both healthy and wealthy.

The Midrash records a conversation between God and the angel who did battle with Ya'akov. God said to the angel, "You made my Cohen (Ya'akov) to have a blemish." The angel responded, "By causing Ya'akov to have a physical defect I was doing him a favor."

What favor did the angel do for Ya'akov?

Esau was angry with Ya'akov because he felt that Ya'akov had stolen the birthright and Ya'akov would serve in the temple and he would not. Now that he saw that Ya'akov had a limp, Ya'akov would not be able to serve in the temple and that appeased Esau's anger. Therefore, when they met, Esau embraced Ya'akov.

Therefore, the verse says that when Ya'akov came to Shechem, he was healed of his limp; his finances were also intact. Then the verse says, "Ya'akov built an altar." Since he was healed, he once again had the status of a Cohen, and he could bring sacrifices.

But with this, however, we will consent to you, if you will be like
us to circumcise every male. (Bereishit 34:15)

Why did the sons of Ya'akov want the men to circumcise themselves?

After they circumcised themselves, Ya'akov's two sons—Shimon and Levi—killed the men of Shechem. Shimon and Levi knew that the neighboring nations would seek revenge against the children of Ya'akov. However, once they discovered that the men of Shechem had circumcised themselves and embraced the Jewish people, the nations would no longer feel a need or desire to defend these "new" Jewish people.

Vayeishev

This week's Torah reading discusses how the brother's sold Yoseph into slavery and told their father, Ya'akov, that Yoseph had been killed by wild animals.

Note: Yitzchak initially wanted to bless Esau. Ya'akov tricked his father into giving him the blessings that were meant for Esau.

Ya'akov wanted to marry Rachel. Laban, his father-in-law, tricked him, and Ya'akov ended up marrying Leah. After marrying Leah, he then married Rachel.

Ya'akov dwelt in the land where his father lived, in the land of Canaan. (Bereishit 37:1)

Rashi explains that Ya'akov wanted to live a life of tranquility, which did not happen because he was confronted with the episode of Yoseph.

Ya'akov transferred the rights of the firstborn from Reuven (the eldest son of Leah) to Yoseph (the eldest son of Rachel),

The Zohar explains Ya'akov's rationale. Ya'akov wanted to marry Rachel first, and since one's thoughts take precedence over one's actions, it is irrelevant that he married Leah first. Therefore, he transferred the rights of the firstborn from Reuven to Yoseph.

How do we know that one's thoughts take precedence over one's actions? We read that Ya'akov wanted to live in tranquility, the reason being his father, Yitzchak, had blessed him with the dew of the heavens. Dew symbolizes tranquility. Therefore, Ya'akov wanted his father's blessings to be actualized.

Ya'akov wanted to actualize the blessing that was intended for someone else but given to him. This clearly demonstrates that Ya'akov sees action to be superior to thought. If that is the case, why then did he transfer the birthright from Reuven to Yoseph?

Seeing that their father wanted to live in tranquility (action takes precedence over thought) and then gave the firstborn rights to Yoseph (thought takes precedence over action), Ya'akov's sons sold Yoseph into slavery so he would not be considered the firstborn.

This is the meaning of Rashi's statement: Ya'akov wanted to live peacefully (to fulfill his father's blessing); instead, he was confronted with the episode of Yoseph (whom the brothers felt did not deserve the rights of the firstborn since Ya'akov married Leah first and Reuven was born first).

They saw him from a distance (Bereishit 37:18)

In this week's Torah reading, we read of the rift that has developed between Yoseph and his brothers. Yoseph had gone looking for them. The brothers see him from the distance. When the Torah says, "They saw him from a distance," this can be understood to mean that they saw the descendants that would come from Yoseph and they saw one of Yoseph's descendant would be a king of Israel by the name of the Yerovom, who was an extremely wicked king. The brothers felt they should kill Yoseph even though he had done nothing wrong. Since his descendant would be wicked, they thought, *We will be ridding the world of future evil.*

Yehudah suggested they sell Yoseph to the Yishmalites. The reason Yehuda suggested this is because the Yishmalites were descendants of Abraham's son Yishmael. During Yishmael's lifetime, the angel wanted to kill Yishmael because he saw how the descendants of Yishmael would cause great suffering to the Jewish people; however, the Torah tells us that Yishmael's life was spared because, at the present moment, Yishmael was acting appropriately, and we should not take into account what will happen in the future.

Likewise Yehudah was saying that Yoseph should be judged like Yishmael, meaning his life should be spared since he, at present, was a righteous person and they were not concerned with what would happen with his descendants.

Mikeitz

They said, "We, your servants, are twelve brothers, the sons of one man in the land of Canaan" (Bereishit 42:13)

In this week's Torah reading, unbeknown to his brothers, Yoseph had become the second in charge to Pharaoh in Egypt. The brothers had come to Egypt to buy supplies, as there was a famine in the Land of Israel. Yoseph had the brothers brought before him and accused them of being spies. The brothers responded by saying, "the sons of one man."

How does this answer refute Yoseph's allegation that they were spies?

The brothers were saying, "We are all the sons of one man. Not any man but an extraordinarily important man." Generally speaking, spies were chosen from the lower elements of society. Becoming a spy was extremely dangerous, and only someone who was very poor and desperate for money would be willing to risk his life for the payment offered. Furthermore, they were saying, "If we are here to spy out the land, why would our father send all of his sons? It would suffice if he would send a few of us."

And Yehudah said, "What shall we say to my master? What shall we speak, and how shall we exonerate ourselves? God has found your servants' iniquity, both we and the one in whose possession the goblet has been found." But he said, "Far be it from me to do this! The man in whose possession the goblet was found he shall be my slave, but as for you go up in peace to your father." So now, please let your servant stay instead of the boy as a slave to my lord, and may the boy go up with his brothers.
(Bereishit 44:16–17.33)

In this week's Torah reading, Yoseph wants Benyamin to remain as a slave in Egypt, and the rest of the brothers can return Ya'akov to their father.

Yehudah initially says that they will all remain enslaved in Egypt, and then when Yoseph says that only the man who stole the goblet shall remain enslaved, Yehudah confronts Yoseph and becomes very angry with him.

What was behind Yehudah's initial approach that they would all stay and become slaves? Why did Yehudah seemingly have a complete change of heart when he was told that only Benyamin would remain? And, at that point, Yehudah challenges Yoseph and states none of them would remain in Egypt.

Yehudah was aware of what God had told Abraham: "Your children will be enslaved and subjugated for 400 years." Yehudah thought that this was the beginning of the exile, and he was therefore more than happy for his brothers and him to remain in Egypt. Once he heard that Yoseph only wanted Benyamin to remain, he realized that this was not the beginning of the exile; he therefore confronted Yoseph and told him that no one was staying.

Vayigash

Then Yehudah approached him and said, "Please, my lord, let now your servant speak something into my Lord's ears, and let not your wrath be kindled against your servant, for you are like Pharaoh." (Bereishit 44:18)

The Midrash on this verse states that Yehudah confronted Yoseph and told him, "In our Torah, the law is if someone steals something and he doesn't have the ability to pay back what he stole, he is sold into slavery. However, our brother Binyamin has the money to pay back what you said he stole so he shouldn't be sold into slavery."

Why did Yehudah think that sharing with Yoseph the law of the Torah would make any impact on Yoseph's decision to enslave Binyamin?

Yehuda, in fact, said the following to Yoseph: "If you consider us to have the status of a Noahite, and we are incumbent to fulfill the Noahite laws, according to the Noahite law, only children from the same mother have the status of being brothers. If, however, we are from the same father but not the same mother, we are not considered brothers. Our brother Binyamin and we share the same father but not the same mother, so we are not related. Therefore, you should believe us when we testify that Binyamin did not steal the goblet. If you consider us to have the status of Israelites, then according to our law, if Binyamin has the ability to pay back that what was stolen, he would not be sold into slavery."

Equally, Yehudah was scared that Yoseph would judge them not as Noahites nor as Israelites but rather as Egyptians. That is why the verse says, "for you are like Pharaoh." As the Midrash explains, "Just as Pharaoh is a king and doesn't keep his word, so to you. Just as Pharaoh had decreed that a slave cannot rule over Egypt, he still appointed you (even though you were a slave); likewise, even if the Egyptian law is that Binyamin cannot go free, you can change the law and allow him to go free."

Vayechi

When the time drew near for Israel to die, he called his son Joseph and said to him, "If I have now found favor in your eyes, now place your hand beneath my thigh, and you shall deal with me with loving kindness and truth; do not bury me now in Egypt. I will lie with my forefathers, and you shall carry me out of Egypt, and you shall bury me in their grave." And he said, "I will do as you said." Ya'akov said, "Swear to me." So he swore to him, and Ya'akov prostrated himself on the head of the bed.
(Bereishit 47:27–30)

Rashi explains that when Ya'akov tells Yoseph to place his hand under his thigh, he is asking Yoseph to make an oath.

In this week's Torah reading, we read of the passing of Ya'akov and how Ya'akov instructed Yoseph to ensure that he be buried in Israel. Why was it necessary for Ya'akov to request from Yoseph that he take two oaths that he would bury him in Israel?

Secondly, in the Hebrew language, the statement "I will *do* as you said," the word for *I* is written *anochi*; it is superfluous because the verb *do* is written in a manner that indicates Yoseph is speaking and therefore the *I* is unnecessary. Why then does the Torah include the word *I*?

Yoseph told his father, "I definitely want to fulfill your wish and bury you in Israel; however, the ultimate decision is dependent on the approval of Pharaoh." Therefore, Ya'akov asked Yoseph to take a second oath. Ya'akov was impressing upon his son Yoseph that "if you will tell Pharaoh that you took an oath, then Pharaoh will allow you to fulfill your promise."

The seemingly extra use of the Hebrew word for *I*—*anochi*—caused Ya'akov some concern. Yoseph's response to his father's initial request was "I [also] will do as you said," meaning I too will request for my corpse to be buried in Israel. Ya'akov knew that Yoseph's coffin would only be taken out from Egypt at the time of the exodus. There-fore, Ya'akov insisted that Yoseph make a second oath because he did not want his body to remain in Egypt until the exodus occurred.

Let my soul not enter their counsel (Bereishit 49:6)

Note: In the times of Moshe, when the Jewish people wanted to enter the Land of Israel, Moshe sent spies to spy out the land. Of the twelve spies sent, ten came back with a negative report.

This verse is part of the blessing that Ya'akov gave to his sons Shimon and Levi. The Talmud (Sanhedrin 109b) is referring to the sin of the spies.

Why did Ya'akov single out Shimon and Levi in connection with the sin of the spies when in fact ten of the twelve spies spoke negatively about the Land, not just Shimon and Levi?

The verse says:

A man said to his brother, "Let us appoint a leader and let us return to Egypt." (Bamidbar 14:4)

Rashi explains that the Jewish people wanted to serve idols and that was the primary sin of the spies. The Midrash says that whenever the verse says, "a man said to his brother," it is referring to Shimon and Levi. The tribes of Shimon and Levi were the main instigators by the sin of the spies. Therefore, Ya'akov alluded to the sin of the spies specifically by Shimon and Levi.

Shemot

These are the names of the children of Israel (Shemot 1:1)

THE MIDRASH EXPLAINS THAT THIS VERSE is proof that the Jewish people were all righteous. How is this verse proof they were all righteous?

The Midrash writes that Noach's true name was Chanina. The reason he was called Noach, it is said, was because many practiced witchcraft in Noach's generation, and Noach concealed his real name so that these witchcraft practitioners would not be able to curse him because they didn't know his real name.

We find a similar situation recorded in the Talmud concerning Rabbi Chanina ben Dosa, a rabbi of the Talmudic era. During Rabbi Chanina ben Dosa's life, there were practitioners of witchcraft. However, due to Rabbi Chanina ben Dosa's righteousness, he was not affected by the witchcraft and there was no need for Rabbi Chanina ben Dosa to change his name, unlike Noach who had to change his name to be protected from the witchcraft.

The Egyptians were known for their prowess in witchcraft, even so the Jewish people didn't change their names as the verse says, "these are the names of the children of Israel." How then were they protected? We must say they were all righteous, similar to Rabbi Chanina ben Dosa, and therefore they did not need to change their names.

And they saw him (Moshe at his birth) and he was good
(Shemot 2:2)

The Midrash brings three opinions in understanding what the Torah means when it says concerning Moshe, "and he was good."

Rabbi Meir says his name was *ki tov*, meaning he was good. Rabbi Nechemiah says that he was born circumcised, and "Others" say that when Moshe was born, the house lit up from Moshe's radiance.

At face value, this Midrash presents three different opinions of three different rabbis.

The Talmud (Eruvin 13b) says that Rabbi Nechemiah's real name is Rabbi Meir. Clearly Rabbi Meir and Rabbi Nechemiah are one and the same.

The Talmud (Horayot 13b) says that whenever the Talmud quotes an opinion in the name of "Others," it is the opinion of Rabbi Meir. Clearly, Rabbi Meir and Others are one and the same. These three rabbis are really one person, Rabbi Meir.

How then can one rabbi (Rabbi Meir) give three different opinions on what the verse means when it says, "and he was good"? We can resolve this question based on the following:

1. A boy should be given his name on the day he is circumcised as we see that God changed Abram's name to Abraham on the day Abraham was circumcised.

2. During the six days of creation, God created light. God, however, concealed that light, and it will only be revealed to the righteous in the Messianic era. This light, however, is revealed to a boy on the day of his circumcision.

Moshe was given the Hebrew name *ki tov* on the day that he was born (Rabbi Meir's opinion). Why was he given his name at birth? Shouldn't he be named at his circumcision?

He was born circumcised (Rabbi Nechemiah's opinion); therefore, he was given his name at birth. If he was born circumcised, would he not see the light from creation that is revealed on the day of circumcision? Therefore, the Torah tells us, even though he did not require circumcision, the house lit up due to Moshe's radiance. The three opinions are intertwined, one with the other.

Va'eira

But Moses spoke before the Lord, saying, "Behold, the children of Israel did not hearken to me. How then will Pharaoh hearken to me, seeing that I am of closed lips?" (Shemot 6:12)

This week's Torah reading discusses Moshe's meeting with Pharaoh. Prior to going, Moshe felt that he was not the appropriate person to represent the Jewish people. He said, "I am of closed lips."

Why did Moshe feel that, since he was of closed lips, Pharaoh wouldn't listen to him?

In Yeshayahu 6:8, it is written:

And I heard the voice of the Lord, saying, "Whom shall I send, and who will go for us?" And I said, "Here I am; send me."

Rashi explains that the verse says "whom shall I send" to admonish the people of Israel. "I sent Amos, and they called him Pesilus because he was tongue-tied."

The commentaries ask why Amos was the one to be sent if he was unable to speak properly.

The level of a person's ability to prophesize is very much dependent on the spiritual level of the Jewish people at the time. In the times of Amos, the Jewish people were idol worshippers and therefore Amos was tongue-tied.

Similarly, Moshe thought if Pharaoh would see that he was of closed lips, he would believe the reason this is so is because the Jewish people are idol worshippers and they are on a very low spiritual level. Pharaoh would then not want to let the people go.

But Moses spoke before the Lord, saying, "Behold, the children of Israel did not hearken to me. How then will Pharaoh hearken to me," (Shemot 6:12)

Note: There are thirteen rules that the rabbis used to derive laws from the words of the Torah. The first rule is a kal vachomer. This means when the Torah says a rule regarding a lenient case (kal), we learn that the rule would certainly apply in a stricter case (chomer). By way of example, if a mother doesn't allow her ten-year-old to cross a busy street on his own, then most definitely we can assume she would not let her five-year-old cross the same busy street by himself.

Rashi explains that this is one of the ten *kal vachomers* mentioned in the Torah. The explanation being that if the Jewish people who are descendants of Abraham, Yitzchak, and Ya'akov and who believe in God will not listen to Moshe, then a nonbelieving ruler such as Pharaoh would most definitely not listen to him.

This line of reasoning doesn't seem to be correct. The reason the Jewish people would not believe in God is specifically mentioned in this section. The verse says:

> *Moshe related this to the children of Israel, but they did not listen to Moshe due to shortness of breath and hard labor.*
> (Shemot 6:9)

The Jewish people didn't listen to Moshe because of their hard labor, something that wasn't applicable to Pharaoh. Perhaps then Pharaoh would listen to Moshe?

The Midrash explains that when the Torah says, "hard labor," it is referring to idol worship, which is hard to break away from. The verse should be understood to mean that the Jewish people did not listen to Moshe because they were idol worshippers.

Pharaoh considered himself an idol.

The *kal vachomer* is this: If the Jewish people who are only serving idols did not listen to Moshe, then Pharaoh who considers himself to be an idol will most definitely not listen to him.[2]

---

2. *Midrash Yehonatan*

Bo

Note: In the Hebrew language, a verb is written in a way that is in sync with the noun it is connected to. For example, I will harden, she will harden, and they will harden. *In each of these examples, the verb* harden *is written differently. Further, in the Torah, there are no punctuation marks.*

Go to Pharaoh because I have hardened his heart (Shemot 10:1)

The verb *harden* is written as *hichbadati*, which translates to mean *I have hardened*. Why then did the Torah have to add the word *ani*, which means *I*?

The question is asked: Why did God resend Moshe to Pharaoh after Pharaoh had declared:

The Lord is the righteous one, and I and my people are the guilty ones. (Shemot 9:27)

The verse is normally read: "The lord is the righteous one, and I" etc., where the comma is placed after the words "righteous one." This implies that Pharaoh is acknowledging that only God is righteous, while he and his people are wicked. However, Pharaoh did not place the comma after the righteous one; rather, he placed it after the words "and I." This implies that Pharaoh believed that he was as holy as God and only his people were guilty. Therefore, Moshe had to return and warn Pharaoh, as he was still wicked.

We now understand the reason it was necessary to insert the word *ani*, I, in the verse, "Go to Pharaoh because I have hardened his heart."

Moshe returned to warn Pharaoh because his heart was still hardened against God. How do we know this? Because in the second verse quoted, Pharaoh said *ani*, I, am righteous like God.

Note: When the Jewish people settled in the Land of Israel, once every seven years all the Jewish people, including the children, had to gather by the temple where they would hear sections of the Torah that spoke about the oneness and the sovereignty of God. This gathering was called **Hakhel**.

> *Moshe said, "With our youth and our elders we will go. With our sons and with our daughters, with our flocks and with our cattle we will go for it is a festival of God for us."* (Shemot 10:9)

This week's Torah reading continues to deal with the confrontation between Moshe and Pharaoh. There is an ongoing argument between the two concerning who Pharaoh is willing to let leave Egypt. At one point, Moshe says, "We are all leaving from our oldest to our youngest."

Moshe informs Pharaoh that *all* the Jewish people will be leaving. The reason being: "We will be celebrating the festival that speaks about the unity of God and His Torah. Therefore we must all go, including the children. Just as by the commandment of *Hakhel* even the children had to participate. Likewise, when we leave Egypt, we will be publicizing God and His Torah and everyone must be there."

Beshalach

Moshe took Yoseph's bones with him (Shemot 13:19)

In this week's Torah reading, we read of the exodus from Egypt. Prior to leaving, Moshe went to gather the bones of Yoseph with him. Why did Moshe feel he was responsible to take Yoseph's coffin more so than anyone else?

Yoseph was sold by his brothers, which ultimately led Yoseph to being enslaved in Egypt, which in turn caused Ya'akov and his family to descend down to Egypt. Of all Yoseph's brothers, it was Shimon and Levi who were the driving force behind Yoseph's sale. Moshe was a descendent of Levi; he therefore felt it was incumbent on him to rectify the error of his ancestor and take Yoseph's bones back to Israel.

He (Pharaoh) took six hundred select chariots and all the chariots of Egypt with officers over them. (Shemot 14:7)

The Jewish people were cursed that one enemy soldier would capture 1,000 Jewish men. Pharaoh thought that the curse began in his times. Since 600,000 men left Egypt, he took 600 soldiers, as each soldier would be able to capture a thousand Jewish men. Besides the 600,000 men, there was also the tribe of the Levites, which numbered 22,000 men.

Pharaoh therefore took officers over them. How many officers did he take? The Torah uses the word *sholishim* for officers. The word *sholishim* can also be translated to mean one-thirtieth. One-thirtieth of 600 is 20. Pharaoh and his personal officer correspond to the extra 2,000. That is why Pharaoh took 620 soldiers besides his personal officer and himself.

Yitro

And Yitro, the prince of Midian, heard (Shemot 18:1)

Why does the Torah need to inform us that Yitro, the father-in-law of Moshe, was the prince of Midian?

The Talmud (Yevamot 24b) states that, during the times of Moshe, King Solomon, and Moshiach, converts would not be accepted by the Jewish people. The reason given is that in these three periods of time, the Jewish people will be living in peace and tranquility and perhaps the reason the individual is converting is not due to his desire to embrace God but rather because being Jewish would allow him to have a peaceful life.

The Talmud asks, if this is so, how did King Solomon allow the daughter of Pharaoh to convert to Judaism?

The Talmud answers that since she was the daughter of a king, she wasn't converting because she wanted to live a peaceful life, as undoubtedly she was already living such a life. Likewise, since Yitro was a prince, he lived a peaceful tranquil life. Therefore, his sole purpose for converting was to embrace God and His Torah.

Note: In Biblical times, people would name their children after events that had impacted their lives.

> *And her two sons, one of whom was named Gershom, because he [Moshe] said, "I was a stranger in a foreign land," And one who was named Eliezer, because [Moshe said,] "The God of my father came to my aid and rescued me from Pharaoh's sword."*
> (Shemot 18:3–4)

In this week's Torah reading, we are told that Moshe's wife, Tzipora, returned to Moshe and the Jewish people. We are also introduced to Moshe's two sons and their names.

Moshe named his first son Gershom. The name Gershom can be read as two words *ger*, which means *a stranger*, and *shom*, which means *there*. Moshe was declaring that he was living in Midian, a foreign land.

His second son was called Eliezer, which can also be divided into two words: *Eli*, which means *my God*, and *Ezra*, which means *came to my aid*. Moshe was referring to the time when he was a young child and God saved his life in Pharaoh's palace. This miracle occurred prior to Moshe's going to live in Midian.

The question is posed: Why didn't Moshe name his first son Eliezer since God's having saved him in Pharaoh's palace occurred prior to his living in Midian?

A true leader of the Jewish people cannot bare seeing the Jewish people suffer. They would rather pass away than witness the Jewish nation suffering pain and anguish.

When Moshe was naming his first child, he was unaware how much longer the Jewish people would be enslaved in Egypt. He therefore felt it would have been better that he had not been saved so many years before by God. He therefore did not want to name his first child Eliezer, which would indicate that he was grateful that God had spared his life.

However, Moshe's second son was born after God had appeared to him at the burning bush and had instructed him to return to Egypt to save the Jewish people. Hearing such good news, he felt he could rightfully name his second son Eliezer, thereby thanking God for saving his life.

> When Moshe's father in law saw what he was doing to the people, he said, "What is this thing you are doing to the people? Why do you sit by yourself, while all the people stand before you from morning till evening?" Moshe said to his father in law "For the people come to me to seek God." (Shemot 18:14–15)

Note: A court case can be decided by following the letter of the law (such a case is called **din**), or it can be decided based on compromise (known as **pesharah**). A case judged using the **din** method must have three judges, *while a* pesharah *needs only one judge. In a case of* din, *the judges sit and the witnesses stand; by* pesharah, *everyone sits. In the case of* din, *if both parties agree, they can have their case adjudicated by one judge.*

The conversation between Yitro and Moshe was based on the laws pertaining to resolving conflict either by the format of din or the format of pesharah. Yitro asked Moshe if he would be judging the case based on din; if so, he should not be sitting alone but as a panel of three judges. He then asked Moshe if he would be judging the case based on pesharah, which would mean that the case could be judged by a single judge. He further asked why the litigants were standing when the law says that the litigants can be seated when judging based on pesharah.

Moshe replied that he was judging the cases based on din; therefore, the litigants needed to stand. He further stated that the law says that when both litigants request it, a case of din can be judged by one judge; you don't need three judges. "Therefore," he said, "I am able to sit in judgment as one judge."

Do not ascend on steps (Shemot 20:23)

How should a judge conduct himself? A judge may feel that the correct approach is to act in a very exalted manner, as King Solomon writes in Mishlei (Proverbs) 29:4:

A king establishes the country with justice.

A judge should act as a king. Similarly, the Talmud (Ketubot 103b) states:

Cast fear upon the students so that they will be in awe of you.

This approach is incorrect. The correct approach is for the judge to act in a very humble manner. This is derived from the following:

The Torah teaches us in Shemot 20:23 that there were no steps leading up to the altar; rather, there was a ramp. In the very next verse, the Torah states, "These are the laws you shall place before them." The

Talmud (Sanhedrin 7b) derives from this that a judge should not step over the heads of the holy people. When students are sitting on the ground to hear a discourse and the judge is attempting to reach his place, it would seem as if he were walking over them.

Rashi, on the verse "And these are the laws you shall place before them," writes just as the earlier *mitzvot* (commandments) were given at Mount Sinai, so too these laws (that the Torah will list) were also given at Mount Sinai.

From the above Talmudic text, we see that the verse "These are the laws you shall place before them" speaks about judges. According to Rashi, this verse incorporates within it the symbolism of Mount Sinai—humility. Therefore, a judge needs to act with humility.[3]

---

3. *Tiferet Yehonatan*

Mishpatim

Note: Prior to the Jewish people receiving the Torah on Mount Sinai, they received a number of laws. One of the laws they received was the need to establish an equitable and fair justice system.

> *And these are the laws you shall place before them. If you acquire a Jewish slave six years he shall be enslaved and in the seventh he will go free. (Shemot 21:1–2)*

As was the case at the time of the exodus, a slave had no recourse to a court of law. His master was his judge and jury. The Jewish people experienced this when they were enslaved in Egypt.

In this week's Torah reading, coming directly after the giving of the Torah on Mount Sinai, God shares many laws that deal with the interaction of society in great detail. The very first set of laws deal with slavery.

When the Jewish people left Egypt prior to receiving the Torah on Mount Sinai, they were instructed to establish a judicial system and received the instruction to do so, they were under the impression that God was signifying to them that they were truly free. Proof of that was the need to establish courts of law, which was totally foreign to a slave. They also felt that these laws were set in order to create an ethical and moral society. And once the Torah was given, there would no longer be a need for laws that seemingly deal with the day-to-day running of society.

Therefore, immediately after the giving of the Torah, the Jewish people received the laws of slavery to impress upon them that there is a deeper and more sublime meaning and message to these laws beyond the need for a just and moral society.

> *These are the laws that you shall place before them.*
> *If you will acquire a Jewish slave (Shemot 21:1–2)*

Why were the laws of slavery the first set of laws given to the Jewish people after receiving the Torah on Mount Sinai?

A slave possessed no rights; he was subservient to the whims and wishes of his master. When the Jewish people were enslaved in Egypt, they also had no rights. However, now that they had received the Torah, they were truly a free people. The Jewish people felt there was no longer a need to have laws pertaining to slavery and the like.

Therefore, after the Torah explained the manner in which the Torah was given, it began listing those mitzvot that were not applicable at the time—to impress upon the Jewish people that all mitzvot have a deeper and a more spiritual dimension. And while the simplistic understanding of the mitzvah is no longer applicable, the spiritual understanding of the mitzvah remains relevant for all times.[4]

When you lend money to My people, to the poor person who is with you (Shemot: 22:24)

Why does the Torah mention "My people" and "the poor person" in the same verse? Why by the poor person does it state, "who is with you"?

The Talmud (Bava Metzia 75b) states that one should always have witnesses present when lending someone money, so when it comes to collecting the loan, the lender will be able to present the witnesses if the borrower refuses to pay.

In Mishlei (Proverbs) 24:14, it is also written:

A gift in secret will appease wrath.

Rashi explains that the word *gift* is referring to charity. We can explain the verse to mean the following: "When you lend money," if you want to lend someone money you should lend the money in the presence of "My people," meaning in front of witnesses. If, however, you want to give charity "to the poor person," you should give it "to the poor person who is with you," when no one else is present.

---

4. *Tiferet Yehonatan*

Terumah

Note: The Tabernacle was 10 cubits high.

This week's Torah reading discusses the building of the Tabernacle. The Midrash states that God asked Moshe to choose priests to serve in the Tabernacle. Moshe asked God from which tribe he should choose from.

God answered, "From the tribe of Levi."

Moshe then asked God, "How should I anoint them?"

God answered, "With the anointing oil."

Moshe said, "How precious is the tribe of the Levites."

After hearing that he was to anoint them with the anointing oil, why did Moshe come to the conclusion that the tribe of the Levites were precious in God's eyes?

The Talmud (Bechoros 44a) states that Moshe and the tribe of Levites were 10 cubits high.

The Mizrachi (Rabbi Eliyahu Mizrachi, 1455–1525) says that King Saul was very tall, and the reason he was taller than everyone else was because he was anointed with the anointing oil. It would seem that the nature of this oil is to make people taller. If that were the case, would the Levites, who were already 10 cubits tall, be taller than the Tabernacle if they were anointed with the oil, and, if so, how would they be able to enter the Tabernacle? The Mizrachi answers that it was a miracle that the Levites, who were taller than 10 cubits, could enter a structure that was 10 cubits high.

Generally speaking, we try to limit the number of miracles. Should God have then chosen another tribe to serve in the Tabernacle? If God would have instructed Moshe to choose another tribe, he wouldn't have asked how he should anoint them as he would have known to use the anointing oil and even though it would mean they would grow taller, they still would have been able to enter the Tabernacle.

However, now that God said to choose the Levites, Moshe asked what he should anoint them with, since he knew that if he anointed them with the anointing oil, they would be taller than the Tabernacle, and God would have to perform a miracle to allow them to enter the Tabernacle. It must be because God cherished the Levites and wanted to choose them even though it would mean that He would have to perform miracles.

And you shall take for me Terumah (Shemot 25:2)

The Midrash, on this verse, quotes from Divrei Hayamim (Chronicles) 29:11:

Yours, O Lord, are the greatness, and the might, and the glory, and the victory, and the majesty

What is the connection between the verse "and you shall take for me" and the verse quoted in the Midrash?

A man can marry a woman in three ways. One of the ways is by giving her something of financial value like a wedding ring. The rabbis explain that God likewise married the Jewish people, and one of the ways was by giving something of value.

Our verse that speaks of the Jewish people giving a gift to God is the manner in which God becomes betrothed to the Jewish people. The obvious question is: God is the male and the Jewish people are the female, should it be God giving us a gift and not we giving God a gift?

The Talmud (Kiddushin 8a) states that if the man is of great importance in such a case that the woman gives the gift to the man and he accepts the gift from her, she is considered to be his betrothed. The reason given is that the pleasure and satisfaction the woman receives because the man accepted her gift is as if the man had given her something of value, and they are considered betrothed. Likewise, when we give a gift to God and God acknowledges the gift and accepts it, that establishes the union between God and the Jewish people.

That is why the Midrash quotes a verse that sings the praises of God to explain why the union is established between God and the Jewish people when the Jewish people are the ones giving the gift.

Tetzaveh

Note: Of the Ten Commandments, God said the first two and the rest where transmitted via Moshe. Likewise, the rest of the Torah was given via Moshe.

And you shall command the children of Israel that they shall bring to you clear olive oil, crushed for lighting, to ignite the lamp continually. (Shemot 27:20)

The verse is referring to the lighting of the menorah, the candelabra. The menorah and its lights symbolize Torah. The verse says, *"crushed for lighting."* Just as the oil used for the menorah needs to be crushed, if someone wants to acquire Torah, he needs to study with great diligence, toil, and effort.

The verse continues and says, "to ignite the lamp continually." This alludes to the fact that one must be completely devoted to one's studies to be constantly learning; otherwise, one would come to forget the Torah one has learned.

If the Jewish people would have merited to receive the Torah directly from God, then they would have merited to never forget it, and they would not have needed to exert tremendous effort to thoroughly understand the Torah.

This is seen in the opening words of the verse, "And you shall command," since Moshe is instructing the Jewish people and not God, they therefore need to crush the oil, symbolizing the need to study intensely something that would be unnecessary if they had received the commandments from God.

Ki Tisa

Note: According to the Torah, if a food that is non-kosher becomes mixed with similar kosher items, such as a non-kosher slice of cheese becomes mixed with kosher slices of cheese, as long as there are more kosher slices than non-kosher, all the slices can be eaten. If, however, the non-kosher item is something that is not sold by weight but because of its importance is sold per item becomes mixed with a similar kosher item, the non-kosher item does not become nullified.

> *When you take the sum of the children of Israel according to their numbers* (Shemot 30:12)

The Midrash quotes a verse in Tehillim (Psalms) 3:3–4:

> *Many men say concerning my soul, "He has no salvation in God to eternity. But you O Lord are a shield about me."*

The Midrash concludes by quoting the verse:

> *When you take the sum of the children.*

What is the Midrash trying to teach us?

The Talmud (Tamid) states that a heretic asked a rabbi, "Why don't you (the Jewish people) become idol worshippers. Doesn't it say in the Torah that we should follow the majority?"

The rabbi responded, "The Jewish people have the status of being an object that is counted and any item that is counted is never nullified."

This conversation is alluded to in the Midrash:

"Many men" (the nations of the world) say, "He has no salvation in God" (and therefore they serve idols). However, the Jewish people say, "You O Lord are a shield about me" (and we do not serve idols). And why don't we follow the majority of mankind and follow the rest of the world? Because we are a people that have been counted "when you take the sum of the children." (We do not become nullified amongst the nations of the world and we only serve God.)

Vayakhel

This is the matter that God commanded. (Shemot 35:4)

This week's Torah reading discusses the building of the Tabernacle.

By the building of the Tabernacle, the verse says, "This is the matter." Earlier in this section, the verse says, "These are the matters." (Shemot 35:1). Why does the Torah change from the plural *these* to the singular *this?*

In the earlier instance, we are discussing the laws of Shabbat. The laws of Shabbat are mentioned very briefly in the Torah and are elaborated in great length in the oral tradition. Therefore, the verse says these in the plural, alluding to both the written and oral tradition.

The building of the Tabernacle is elaborated in great detail in the Torah in the written tradition. Therefore, the word *this* in the singular is used.

Another approach in explaining the use of a singular or plural word is as follows: By the building of the Tabernacle, there is only one positive commandment; therefore, the word *this* is used. The laws of Shabbat contain a positive and a negative commandment; therefore, the word *these* is used.

Pikudei

*These are the accounts of the tabernacle, the tabernacle
of testimony (Shemot 38:21)*

This week's Torah reading gives us the calculation of all the donations given for the construction of the Tabernacle. Why is the Tabernacle referred to as the Tabernacle of testimony? What was the Tabernacle testifying about?

The Tabernacle was testifying that God was placing His glory on the Jewish people. This was evident from the constant miracles that occurred in the Tabernacle on a daily basis.

Rashi explains that the testimony was that God had forgiven the Jewish people and had also forgiven the foreign nations that joined the Jewish people at the time of the exodus.

How do we know that God had forgiven the mixed multitude?

The Torah tells us that every Jew had to give a half a shekel to help build the Tabernacle. In this week's reading, we have listed exactly what the half shekel was used for. Based on the calculations, it is evident that the mixed multitude did not contribute by giving a half a shekel. Even so, they were permitted to enter the Tabernacle. This is a clear indication that they had also been forgiven.

*Bezalel, son of Uri, son of Hur, of the tribe of Yehudah, had
made all that the Lord had commanded Moshe. With him was
Oholiab, son of Ahisamach, of the tribe of Dan, a craftsman
and master weaver, and an embroiderer in blue, purple, and
crimson wool in linen. (Shemot 38:22–23)*

Rashi explains that Moshe had commanded Bezalel to first make the furnishing and afterward the Tabernacle. Bezalel responded, "It is common practice to first make a house and then put in the furniture." Bezalel first built the Tabernacle, and then he made the vessels.

It is well known that the gold used in making the vessels were an atonement for the sin of the golden calf and the idol of Michah, while the silver used was an atonement for the sale of Yoseph.

Moshe and Bezalel each wanted the Tabernacle to be built so that it would bring atonement for their tribe's transgression.

Bezalel was from the tribe of Yehudah. Yehudah was instrumental in the sale of Yoseph. Therefore, Bezalel wanted to construct the Tabernacle first, since silver was used in its construction.

Moshe wanted the vessels to be built first to atone for the sin of the golden calf, since Moshe felt he needed to atone for the sin of the golden calf—the reason being that Moshe had allowed the mixed multitude to leave Egypt together with the Jewish people, and it was the mixed multitude who were responsible for the golden calf.

Oholiab devoted himself in making the garments. The garments contained a lot of gold. Oholiab was from the tribe of Dan, and the tribe of Dan was responsible for the idol of Michah.

Vayikra

Note: The letters in the Torah are of a standard size; however, sometimes certain letters are written larger or smaller than standard. Commentators try to explain the reason for the discrepancy.

And He called to Moshe (Vayikra 1:1)

This week's Torah reading discusses the various sacrifices that were brought in the Tabernacle.

The Hebrew word for *called* is *vayikra*. The last letter of the word *vayikra* is an *aleph*—the first letter of the Hebrew alphabet. The aleph is written much smaller than the rest of the word.

When Moshe was about to descend with the first set of tablets after the Jewish people sinned with the golden calf, God said to Moshe, "You shall descend" (Shemot 32:7), meaning from your greatness.

Why should Moshe's spiritual level be diminished because the Jewish people sinned? The answer given is because Moshe, to a certain extent, was responsible for the golden calf. Why?

When the Jewish people left Egypt, God only wanted the Jewish people to leave. Moshe, however, decided to allow the mixed multitude to join in the exodus. It was the mixed multitude who made and danced around the golden calf. Moshe was therefore somewhat responsible for what had occurred.

The Torah wrote the letter *aleph* smaller than all the other letters to emphasize that Moshe's greatness was somewhat diminished.

Speak to the children of Israel, and say to them: When a man from (among) you brings a sacrifice to the Lord (Vayikra 1:2)

The Midrash states, "You and not Moshe." The Midrash seems to imply that Moshe was not permitted to bring a sacrifice, which is difficult to understand. How then should we understand the Midrash?

The Talmud (Nedarim 10a) states that when a person wants to bring a sacrifice to the Temple he should not say "to God a sacrifice"; rather, he should say "a sacrifice to God." Why is this so?

If a person would say, "to God a sacrifice," perhaps after the person said, "to God," he would pass away and then he would have said the name of God in vain.

This law is learned from our verse that concludes with the phrase "a sacrifice to the Lord," and it did not say, "to the Lord a sacrifice."

Moshe knew when he would be passing away; therefore, Moshe would be permitted to say *to the Lord a sacrifice*, since he knew he would not pass away after saying "to the Lord."

This is the understanding of the Midrash when it says, *you and not Moshe*. It is not excluding Moshe from bringing a sacrifice. Rather, it is coming to teach us that the law of not saying "to the Lord a sacrifice" is not applicable to Moshe.[5]

---

5. *Midrash Yehonatan*

Tzav

Command Aaron and his sons, saying (Vayikra 6:2)

Rashi explains that this commandment involved a financial loss; therefore, the word *command* was used because the word *command* means a person should act diligently, and when there is a financial loss involved, a person may not be that keen to fulfill God's instruction; therefore, the Torah used the word *tzav*, which means *command*.

What financial loss would the Cohanim have by offering the various sacrifices? The daily sacrifices were purchased with money that had been donated to the Tabernacle.

We can answer this question through understanding a Midrash.

The Midrash states that throughout the Torah reading of Vayikra, no reference is made to Aaron. The Torah addresses the sons of Aaron but not Aaron himself. Why is this so?

There is another Midrash that states that while the Jewish people were in the desert, the only sacrifice that was offered on the altar was the *olat tamid* (the daily fully burnt sacrifice). The section of Vayikra discusses many sacrifices that were brought only once the Jewish people entered Israel. Aaron passed away in the desert. As a result, he never had the opportunity to bring any of the sacrifices mentioned in the section of Vayikra. Therefore, the Torah does not address him in the section of Vayikra and only addresses his children who entered the Land of Israel and would bring all the other types of sacrifices.

In the section where the Torah is discussing the daily fully burnt sacrifice that was offered in the desert, the Torah makes reference to Aaron as well since Aaron offered the daily fully burnt sacrifices in the desert.

There is an opinion that says that the Cohanim paid for the daily fully burnt sacrifice in the desert. This will resolve our question why the Torah used the word *command*.

In the desert, only one sacrifice was offered, and that sacrifice was paid for by the Cohanim. Since this involved a financial loss, the Torah had to say, "command Aaron and his sons."

Shemini

And Aaron's sons, Nadav and Avihu, each took his pan
(Vayikra 10:1)

The Talmud (Sanhedrin 52a) states that while Moshe and Aaron were walking, they were being followed by Nadav and Avihu. Finally, when the rest of the Jewish people were also walking, Nadav said to Avihu, "When will these two old men pass away and you and I will rule?"

Why did Nadav and Avihu believe that they would succeed Moshe and Aaron as the next leaders of the Jewish people?

When Ya'akov blessed his children prior to his passing, he blessed Yehuda with the following blessing:

The scepter shall not depart from Yehudah nor the student of the law from between his feet (Bereishit 49:10)

We learn from this verse that the kings of Israel will be descendants of Yehudah.

Ramban explains that this is the reason why the Chashmonoim (Maccabees) who had taken the kingship away from the tribe of Yehudah met such a tragic end. The Chashmonoim were not from the tribe of Yehudah, and they had no right to appoint the king from their family.

Based on Ramban, what right would Nadav and Avihu have to become the leaders of the Jewish people as they were not from the tribe of Yehudah?

We find in Jewish history that the rabbis took the position of leadership away from Rabbi Gamliel, and they gave it to Rabbi Elazar ben Azariah. Rabbi Gamliel was from the tribe of Yehudah, and Rabbi Elazar ben Azariah was not. How could the rabbis transfer the leadership position to a rabbi not from the tribe of Yehudah?

Finally, the family of the Chashmonoim were great and righteous people. Were they not aware of Ya'akov's blessing to Yehudah?

The Talmud (Sanhedrin 5b) explains that when the verse says, "the student of the law from between his feet," this refers to the descendants of Hillel who were from the house of King David. Tosafot explains that the descendants of Hillel were from the house of King David only via matrimonial descent. According to Tosafot, one can be considered a descendant of the tribe of Yehudah in respect to a position of leadership even if it is only via the mother.

All the Cohanim are descendants of Aaron. Aaron's wife was the sister of Nachshon ben Aminadav, who was a descendant of Yehudah. Therefore, every Cohen is a descendant via his mother from the tribe of Yehudah.

Rabbi Elazar ben Azariah was a Cohen; therefore, he was also a descendant from the tribe of Yehudah. Therefore, the rabbis were able to transfer the position of leadership to him. Similarly, the Chashmonoim were Cohanim: they too had the right to be leaders of the Jewish people.

Nadav and Avihu said, "Moshe and Aaron are not descendants of Yehudah. They should not be the leaders of the Jewish people; however, we are descendants of the tribe of Yehudah and therefore we should lead the Jewish people."

Note: When King Solomon inaugurated the First Temple, he and the Jewish people celebrated for seven days. The seven days overlapped Yom Kippur. Normally, one is obligated to fast on Yom Kippur; however, that year King Solomon felt that Yom Kippur could be set aside.

This week's Torah reading discusses the erecting of the Tabernacle.

The Midrash states that we need to compare the number seven to the number eight, meaning just as Moshe built the Tabernacle in eight days, those eight days were without sin. Likewise, the seven days that King Solomon dedicated the First Temple were without sin.

The Midrash is informing us that during the eight days of erecting the Tabernacle, sacrifices were brought every day. This included

Shabbat. Outside of the service of the Tabernacle, slaughtering an animal and other acts necessary in preparing an animal for a sacrifice would be prohibited. One would think that during the eight days of preparing the Tabernacle for its service, one couldn't bring sacrifices on the Shabbat. The Midrash informs us that is not the case, and Moshe was permitted to bring the sacrifices.

King Solomon deduced from this the following: If the Tabernacle, which was a temporary structure, was allowed to desecrate the Shabbat during the eight days of the inauguration, then without doubt during the seven days of the inauguration of the First Temple, one would be able to desecrate Yom Kippur and be able to rejoice and have a festive meal on Yom Kippur.

There is a discussion whether the sanctity of the First Temple remained forever even after its destruction or perhaps the sanctity was dependent on the Temple's presence. And when the Temple was destroyed, its sanctity was removed.

King Solomon must have been of the opinion that the sanctity of the Temple was eternal, and the site of the Temple was holy even after its destruction. How do we know this to be the opinion of King Solomon?

King Solomon's reasoning was based on comparing the inauguration of the Tabernacle and the Temple. He said, if the Tabernacle, which was only temporary and could override the sanctity of the Shabbat, the Temple, which is eternal, could definitely override the sanctity of Yom Kippur. Clearly, King Solomon was of the opinion that the Temple's sanctity was eternal. Because if it wasn't eternal, the Temple would be considered a temporary structure, making it no holier than the Tabernacle.

Tazria

Speak to the children of Israel saying, if a woman conceives and gives birth to a male (Vayeira 12:2)

This week's Torah reading begins with the laws of childbirth. The previous section discussed the laws of kashrut, elaborating on the types of creatures a person is permitted to eat and those that a person may not. What is the connection between the section of kashrut and the laws of childbirth? We can resolve this question by understanding another matter.

The question is posed: Why doesn't God create each human being just as God created Adam and Chava? The answer given is: If God would create every human being, there would be no possibility of repenting if one sinned.

The question is also asked: Why did God create all the non-kosher animals? An answer given is: To impress upon the Jewish people, even though the non-kosher animals are not bound by the concepts of reward and punishment, God still sustains them.

Then definitely, God will have compassion on the Jewish people who are bound by reward and punishment and accept their *teshuvah* (repentance).

We will now understand the link between the list of non-kosher animals and childbirth.

If God has compassion on the non-kosher species, then definitely God will have compassion on a human being and accept their *teshuvah*; this would not be the case if the human had been created by God.

And call out, "Unclean! Unclean!" (Vayikra 13:45)

Note: A metzorah *is a person afflicted with* tzora'as. Tzora'as *is a miraculous affliction of the skin that occurred as a punishment for idle talk or gossip.*

The Talmud (Shabbat 67a) learns from this verse that the person stricken with *tzora'as* should inform people what has happened so that they should pray for him. Why does the Torah specifically tell us that one should pray for the person with *tzora'as*? Wouldn't every sick person gain from the prayers of others?

Furthermore the Torah states, "And God heard the voice of the lad." This verse is speaking about Yishmael, who was in dire straits. Rashi points out that we learn from this verse that a sick person who prays for his own health is accepted by God more than if someone else prays for him.

If this is the case, shouldn't the person with *tzora'as* pray on his own behalf?

The person with *tzora'as* is called *musgar* (imprisoned). The rabbis explain this to mean that his prayers are not accepted in heaven. Therefore, the *metzorah* has no other recourse than to ask others to pray for him.[6]

---

6. *Midrash Yehonosan*

Metzora

When you come to the land of Canaan, which I am giving you
as a possession, and I place a lesion of tzara'ath upon a house
in the land of your possession. (Vayikra 14:34)

This week's Torah reading continues to discuss the laws of *tzora'as*
that affects one's body, clothing, or house. The verse quoted is explaining why a person's home would be afflicted with *tzora'as* if the person
only made a minor transgression.

It is well known that if a person had a particular illness, it is easier
for that person to be afflicted again.

The Jewish people moved into the homes of the Canaanim; while
Canaanim lived there, the walls of the houses were filled with impure
objects. Once the Jewish people arrived, they purified the homes. However, even a slight sin would bring the impurities back onto the walls of
the house.

The question can be asked is: If the Canaanim had impurities on
their walls, why didn't the walls have tzora'as?

There is a halachic ruling that a person cannot prohibit something that isn't theirs. The verse stated, "which I am giving *you* as a
possession." The Land of Israel and anything connected to its ground
always belonged to the Jewish people, even before they entered it. The
Canaanim never had ownership of the Land of Israel; they therefore
could not prohibit the homes to be built there because they never
owned it. Therefore, no *tzora'as* could be found on its walls.

Acharei

God spoke to Moshe after the passing of Aaron's two sons when they came near, before God, and they died (Vayikra 16:1)

This week's Torah reading discusses the service that took place on Yom Kippur. The Talmud states that the section discussing the laws of Yom Kippur was spoken on the same day Aaron's two sons died.

There is a rule that whenever the Torah uses the word *after* (in Hebrew *achrei*), it teaches us that a lengthy period of time elapsed between the two events. If that is the case, how do we understand the use of the word *after* in our verse?

The Talmud states that on the same day Aaron's sons died, we were taught the laws of Yom Kippur.

The verse explained the reason they died: "when they came near, before God." Normally, we understand this statement to mean that Aaron's two sons came close to the Tabernacle when they shouldn't have.

However, we can explain that the reason given for why they died was not referring to their coming close to the Tabernacle but to an event that had occurred some six months prior. Moshe descended Mount Sinai on Yom Kippur with the second set of tablets. The Jewish people had been instructed not to come close to Mount Sinai. Aaron's two sons didn't heed this instruction, and they came close to the mountain. They should have died for this transgression. God, however, didn't want to spoil the joy of the Jewish people receiving the tablets by taking the lives of Aaron's two sons. God waited until the building of the Tabernacle many months later.

Based on this explanation, the word *after* in this verse is consistent with its regular understanding in that it is referring to two events that had a large gap between them—in our case, the giving of the Torah and the erecting of the Tabernacle some ten months later.

God spoke to Moshe after the passing of Aaron's two sons when they came near, before God, and they died (Vayikra 16:1)

The Midrash states that when the two sons of Aaron passed away, the angels asked God, "Why did You split the sea for the Jewish people?"

What is the connection between splitting of the Reed Sea and the passing of Aaron's two sons? The commentators explain that Aaron's two sons passed away because Aaron helped in making the golden calf.

The Talmud (Sanhedrin 7a) explains that the people first came to Chur and asked him to make the golden calf, and when he refused, they killed him. They then went to Aaron. Aaron had no choice but to help them or they would have killed him as well.

Even though this was the case, Aaron could not justify his actions by saying he was forced into doing it. Therefore, his two sons passed away.

After seeing Aaron's two sons passing away, the angels realized that being forced into making an idol or serving an idol does not exempt the person from being punished. Therefore, they said to God, "Why are you saving the Jewish people? They are idol worshippers." To which God responded by saying, "The Jewish people had no choice; they were forced."

The angels did not accept God's answer. The angels said, "Aaron's sons died for Aaron's sin even though he was forced. Likewise, the Jewish people should be punished, and the excuse that they were forced is irrelevant."[7]

---

7. *Midrash Yehonatan*

Kedoshim

Note: The mitzvah of Hakhel is that all the Jewish people had to come to the Temple and be addressed by the king.

> _You shall be holy. Because I, God your God, am holy._
> (Vayikra 19:2)

This week's Torah reading presents many laws that comprise the 613 commandments.

Ramban explains the Torah statement "you shall be holy" to mean that one should sanctify one's self even with that which is permitted—meaning one should not overindulge in earthly pleasures even though they may not be prohibited.

From the writings of Josephus, at the time of the Roman occupation of Israel during the Second Temple, many Jewish people isolated themselves in the fields, living like hermits and eating only fruit and vegetables they could find. They literally separated themselves from all worldly pleasures. However, such behavior was frowned upon by the majority of Jewish people living there at the time.

If one wants to serve God properly, it must be service that is pleasant both for man and for God. It must be a form of service that allows the world to continue and flourish. If everyone would be hermits, the world could no longer continue and flourish.

The test if the service is an appropriate one is to determine if the nation would flourish or not if _all_ the Jewish people were to act in such a manner.

This is alluded to in the Midrash. The Midrash states that this section commanding the Jewish people to be holy was said on _Hakhel_ (when all the Jewish people gathered together). To impress upon the person if one is deciding whether one should refrain from a permitted activity, one should ask oneself, "If all the Jewish people would refrain from it, what would be the impact on the nation as a whole?"

You shall be holy (Vayikra 19:2)

The Midrash states that the Jewish people said to God, "You called us holy; remove death from us."

What is the connection between being holy and not dying?

The rabbis explain that the reason people pass away is because God said, "I created mankind from the dust of the earth; therefore mankind must return to the dust of the earth."

The Talmud (Bava Kamma 65b) states that if a person steals an object and the object is now called by a different name when the thief is caught, he does not have to return the actual item that was stolen (since it is now called by another name); he just needs to return the monetary value of the item stolen.

Likewise, the Talmud states that if a person stole an animal and then sanctified it, when the thief is caught, he doesn't have to return the animal since it is now called holy.

The Midrash can be understood to mean the following: Since the Jewish people are now called holy, they no longer need to be returned to where they had come from—meaning they no longer need to return to *the dust of the earth*, and they should not need to pass away.

Emor

Note: When the Torah wants to use the word speak, it will either use the word vayomer or vaydaber. The rabbis explain that if the Torah uses the word vayomer, it means the person is speaking in a pleasant manner. If the Torah uses the word vaydaber, it means the person speaking and the message being conveyed is harsh. Further, a Cohen is not permitted to become impure. One of the ways a Cohen could become impure is by coming in contact with a corpse.

> *And the Lord said to Moses: Speak to the Cohanim, the sons of Aaron, and say to them: Let none [of you] defile himself for a dead person among his people. (Vayikra 21:1)*

This week's Torah reading begins by discussing laws pertaining to the Cohen (the priest).

In the opening verse, the verb *speak* is mentioned twice. The rabbis deduce from this that the adult Cohanim must ensure that the Cohanim who are still minors should not defile themselves by coming in contact with a corpse.

The Torah specifically uses the verb *emor*. Since we are speaking to children, the message will best be conveyed if it is expressed in a very gentle and pleasant manner.

> *And the Lord said to Moses: Speak to the Cohanim, the sons of Aaron. (Vayikra 21:1)*

The Midrash quotes the verse in Tehillim (Psalms) 12:7:

> *The sayings of the Lord are pure sayings.*

What is the connection between the verse "And the Lord said to Moses: Speak to the Cohanim, the sons of Aaron," and the verse quoted in the Midrash?

The Talmud (Berachot 22a) records a discussion between Rabbi Yehudah ben Besera and his student. The student said that he was in a state of impurity and he was unsure whether he could say words of Torah. Rabbi Yehudah told him that words of Torah do not become impure, as the verse says:

My words are like fire said the Lord (Yermiyahu 23:29)

Rabbi Yehudah continued, "Just as fire doesn't become impure, so too words of Torah do not become impure. Therefore, you are permitted to say words of Torah even if you are impure."

The answer Rabbi Yehudah gave to his student will also answer the question that the heretic posed to Rabbi Avahu recorded in the Talmud (Sanhedrin 39a). The heretic asked, "Your God is a Cohen. How did He then purify himself after burying Moshe?"

According to Rabbi Yehudah, the words of Torah can never become impure. If God's words can never become impure, it is self-understood that God himself cannot become impure.

We will now be able to understand the Midrash. The Torah verse said a Cohen is not permitted to become impure. The Midrash is coming to answer the following question: If a Cohen can't become impure, how could God, who has the status of a Cohen, bury Moshe?

The Midrash answers this question by quoting the verse, "The sayings of the Lord are pure sayings." If God's words can't become impure, then He himself cannot become impure and therefore God was allowed to bury Moshe.

Behar

Note: The law of Shmita is that every seventh year in the Land of Israel all the fields needed to remain fallow. One of the reasons given for this commandment was to enable the farmers to dedicate a year to the study of God's Torah.

> *And God spoke to Moshe at Mount Sinai, saying, "Speak to the children of Israel, when you will come to the land that I am giving you, the land should rest a Sabbath for God."*
> (Vayikra 25:1–2)

Rashi wonders why the Torah informed us that the commandment of Shmita was given at Mount Sinai when all the commandments were given at Sinai. Rashi's answer is that it is to impress upon us that, just as all aspects of the commandment of Shmita were given at Sinai, so it is true by all the commandments that the commandment in its entirety were given at Sinai.

The Talmud in Berachot records an argument between Reb Shimon bar Yochai (also known as the Rashbi) and Reb Yishmael. The Rashbi said one should not involve himself in working one's fields; rather, a person should dedicate himself completely to the study of Torah, and the upkeep of his fields will be taken care of by others. Reb Yishmoel said that many have attempted to live by this rule but were unsuccessful.

Tosafot explains that if someone is a *tzaddik* (a completely righteous individual), others will take care of his fields and he can devote his day to Torah study. If he is not a tzaddik, he will have to care for his fields on his own. That is why many attempted but failed to follow the path set forth by the Rashbi—since most people are not completely righteous.

If someone is a truly righteous person, there is no need for the commandment of Shmita as he is always immersed in studying God's

Torah. When the Jewish people were at Mount Sinai and were receiving the Torah prior to the sin of the golden calf, they were all on the level of tzaddikim. That being the case, there would be no need to give the Jewish people the law of Shmita.

This insight will give us a deeper understanding of the question posed by Rashi earlier. Rashi asked, "Why by the law of Shmita does the Torah inform us that it was given at Mount Sinai?"

The question being asked is: When the Jewish people were at Mount Sinai, why was there a need to give the Jewish people the commandment of Shmita? The Jewish people were all righteous and devoted their entirety to the study of God's Torah, and they didn't need to be instructed to vacate their fields once every seven years.

As a result, one might be under the impression that the law of Shmita was not given at Mount Sinai and only given to the Jewish people *after* the sin of the golden calf. Therefore, the Torah specifically states that the law of Shmita was given at Mount Sinai, and it was given conditionally—meaning that if the Jewish people would remain completely righteous then the law of Shmita would not be introduced. If, however, the Jewish people sin and are no longer completely righteous and will have to work their fields, then the law of Shmita will apply.

Bechukotai

Note: The 613 mitzvot (commandments) are divided into various categories. One category is called chukim (statutes), where the reason for the mitzvah is not known to man—such as shatnez the prohibition of wearing a garment of wool and linen.

If you will walk in my statutes (Vayikra 26:3)

Usually, the Torah would say, "If you keep my statutes." Why does the Torah use the word *walk* in connection with mitzvot that are illogical?

The Prophet Zechariah writes:

And I will give you walkers who walk among those that stand still. (Zechariah 3:7)

"Those that stand still" refers to the angels. Why are the righteous referred to as walkers while angels are referred to as those that stand still?

The angels remain standing still; they do not elevate themselves from one level to another. The righteous, on the other hand, are always climbing and elevating themselves from one level to another. Once a righteous person passes away, he remains at the same level that he had reached while alive.

Angels also fulfill God's instructions. Why are the angels unable to elevate themselves from one level to the next like the righteous can?

Angels comprehend the reason for the particular mitzvah that they are commanded in doing; therefore, their reward is not that great. The reward is far greater for the tzaddikim who do not know the reasons for the mitzvah.

Therefore, those laws that fit into the category of *chukim* (illogical commandments), the reward for the tzaddik is far greater. That is why the verse says, "if you will walk in my statutes"— meaning by keeping my statutes (whose reason is concealed), you will ascend from one level to the next.

I will give your rains in their correct time (Vayikra 26:4)

Note: Very often Reb Yehonatan will explain the reason the Torah writes two verses in close proximity one to the other. The previous Torah reading concludes, "You shall keep my Shabbat" (Vayikra 26:2), while the second verse in Bechukotai states, "I will give your rain in their correct time." What is the connection between keeping Shabbat and the correct time for rain to fall?

The Talmud (Shabbat 118b) states that whoever observes the Shabbat, his sins will be forgiven. The Talmud (Taanit 7b) states that rain only falls when the Jewish people's transgressions are forgiven.

Based on these two Talmudic sources, we can understand the connection between the two verses. If Jewish people keep Shabbat, this ensures that our sins are forgiven. Therefore, the Torah then writes, "I will give your rains in their correct time."

Bamidbar

The Lord spoke to Moshe in the Sinai Desert. . . in the second year after the exodus from the land of Egypt. Take the sum of all the congregation . . . a head count of every male
(Bamidbar 1:1–2)

IT WOULD SEEM FROM THESE TWO VERSES that there is a link between the Jewish people leaving Egypt and God's instruction to count the Jewish people.

The commentators ask, "How could God instruct Moshe to count the Jewish people when the Talmud (Taanit 8b) writes, blessing cannot be found on something that was counted?"

The commentators answer is: If the object is holy, God's blessing will be found on something that was counted.

Another question posed is: Why do we thank God for taking us out of Egypt when God had promised Abraham that after 400 years of slavery, we would be taken out of exile?

We thank God not for taking us out, but rather for the manner in which He took us out. He took us out when we were at the forty-ninth level of impurity, and after our exodus, we reached the forty-ninth level of holiness.

We will now be able to understand the link between the exodus and the Jewish people being counted. "The Lord spoke to Moshe in the Sinai Desert . . . in the second year after the exodus from the land of Egypt." Therefore, we had reached a very high level of holiness. As a result, "take the sum of all the congregation," because anything that is holy can be counted and will still receive God's blessing.

These are the names of Aaron's sons . . . These are the names of Aaron's sons (Bamidbar 3:2–3)

This week's Torah reading discusses the tribes and how many males were in each tribe. Why does the Torah repeat, "these are the names of Aaron's sons" one verse after the other?

The custom by idol worshippers was, if a person was elevated to a higher position, they would change their names. The Torah is informing us this was not the case by the Jewish people. The Cohanim did not change their names even though they were elevated to serve in the Tabernacle.

Naso

From those thirty years old and upwards, until fifty years old.
(Bamidbar 4:35)

This week's Torah reading discusses the role of the Levites and the Cohanim.

The Torah taught us that the Jewish male would be drafted into the army from the age of twenty till the age of sixty. Our verse teaches us that the Cohen would serve in the Tabernacle from the age of thirty till the age of fifty. Why didn't the Cohen work in the Tabernacle the same amount of years that the Israelite served in the army?

Every ten years of a person's life correspond to another planet in the galaxy. From the age of twenty till thirty, the planet corresponding to that period of a person's life is *mazal madim* (Mars). *Madim* signifies blood. Therefore, from the age of twenty a person would go to war.

At the age of sixty a person reaches *mazal levana*. *Levana* signifies the moon. The moon has no independent light; it reflects the light of the sun. This signifies a weakening of a person's strength. Therefore, at the age of sixty, the Israelite would no longer go to war.

The Levite began their service once the ten years of *mazal madim* had elapsed. They remained in service till the age of fifty. At the age of fifty, the *mazel kochav*, signifying mercury, begins. Mercury signifies study and intellectual pursuit. The years between fifty and sixty are opportune years to devote to Torah study.

This is seen in Pirkei Avot (Ethics of the Fathers) where it states that at the age of sixty, one is considered old. The word for *old* used is *ziknah*, which is an acronym for *zeh shekanah chachma* (one who has acquired wisdom). By studying from fifty to sixty, when one reaches the age of sixty, one will be a learned individual.

Therefore, the Levites and the Cohanim stopped serving in the Tabernacle and Temple at the age of fifty to enable them to devote their day to the study of Torah.

God will bless you and protect you (Bamidbar 6:24)

The Midrash explains this verse to mean that God will bless you with wealth, and God will protect you from evil spiritual forces. What is the connection between wealth and evil spiritual forces?

The Talmud (Taanit 8b) states that God blesses only those things that cannot be seen.

It is well known that evil forces can cause harm even to things that are hidden. If that is the case, what benefit would a person have from being blessed with wealth? To receive the blessing of wealth, the wealth would have to be concealed, but the evil forces can harm even things that are hidden. Therefore, the verse says, "God will bless you" with wealth. And, if one will ask, "Won't the evil forces be able to harm one's hidden wealth?" the blessing concludes with "and protect you" from the evil spiritual forces.

Beha'alotcha

Note: Moshe's father-in-law's name was Yitro. However, he was known by other names. In the following verse, he is known as Chovav. Rashi explains that the word chovav *means to love, and Yitro was called Chovav because he loved the Torah.*

> *Then Moshe said to Chovav, the son of Reuel the Midianite, Moshe's father-in-law, We are travelling to the place about which the Lord said, I will give it to you. Come with us and we will be good to you, for the Lord has spoken of good fortune for Israel.* (Bamidbar 10:29)

In this verse, we read that God promised the Jewish people that he will give them the Land of Israel as a gift. However, in other places, we read how the Land of Israel is an inheritance of the Jewish people and that we inherited the land from our forefathers Abraham, Yitzchak, and Ya'akov.

We received the Land of Israel both as an inheritance and as a gift. Israel has two aspects to it: the physical and the spiritual.

The physical aspect of the land is its borders and the actual land, which is something that we inherited from our forefathers. The spiritual aspect of the land was given to us as a gift from God. The Talmud describes the spirituality of the land to mean that even though Israel is a small country, miraculously it was able to contain within it a vast amount of people—or that its crop would be ready for harvest very quickly.

Moshe promised Yitro that he and his descendants would inherit land in proximity to the city of Jericho. The rabbis tell us that the actual land was not very large. How then did Moshe think that telling Yitro he was only receiving a small parcel of land would convince him to come?

That is why Moshe told Yitro that the Land of Israel was being given to us a gift. Since it is a gift from God, miraculously a small area of land will be large enough and be able to sustain all your descendants.

Eldad and Medad were prophesizing in the camp.
(Bamidbar 11:27)

Note: Eldad and Medad were prophesizing that Moshe would not enter the Land of Israel. Rather, Moshe's student Yehoshua would take the Jewish people into Israel. Further: Sela was a coin used in Talmudic times. The word sela can also be translated to mean a rock.

The Talmud (Megillah 28a) states that if the spoken word is worth a *sela*, then silence is worth two *selaim*.

The reason Moshe did not take the Jewish people into Israel was because he struck the rock instead of talking to it. We can now understand the Talmudic phrase, "If the spoken word is worth a *sela*, then silence is worth two *selaim*," to be referring to the incident of Eldad and Medad.

"If the spoken word is worth a *sela*": If Moshe would have spoken to the rock instead of hitting it, he would have taken the Jewish people into Israel.

"Then silence is worth two *selaim*": Then the two who had prophesized that Moshe would be replaced by Yehoshua would have had to remain silent, since Moshe would have taken the Jewish people into Israel.

Shelach

Note: Moshe sent twelve spies to spy out the Land of Israel. Of the twelve spies, only Yehoshua and Calev came back with a positive finding. The other ten returned with a negative report. When the spies began to give their negative report, Calev silenced the crowd and spoke positively about Israel.

> *These are the names of the men that Moshe sent to spy out the land. And Moshe called Hoshea Yehoshua.*
> (Bamidbar 13:16)

This week's Torah reading discusses how Moshe sent spies to spy out the Land of Israel.

Why didn't Yehoshua speak out publicly about the virtues of the land as Calev did?

Eldad and Medad were prophesizing that Moshe would not take the people into the land but rather Yehoshua would. Yehoshua was concerned that if he were outspoken, the Jewish people would think he was being self-serving.

If this was what motivated Yehoshua to remain silent, why did Moshe send him in the first place? Wouldn't the Jewish people reject his opinion since they would say, of course, he is giving a positive report because he wants to become the leader of the Jewish people?

Yehoshua was known by everyone as Hoshea. When Eldad and Medad prophesized that Yehoshua would lead the people into the land, they had no idea who they were referring to. Therefore, Moshe saw no problem in sending Yehoshua as no one knew his name had been changed.

Yehoshua, however, was concerned that perhaps people would know or discover that he had a new name, and if he spoke positively about Israel, he would be suspected of self-interest.

Korach

And Korach took (Bamidbar 16:1)

This week's Torah reading deals with the revolt of Korach against Moshe.

The commentators explain that Korach saw that Shmuel Hanavi (Samuel the Prophet) would descend from him. And Shmuel is considered as great as Moshe and Aaron. He therefore felt he would be victorious in his revolt against them.

Why did Korach think that he was suitable for a position of leadership?

The Talmud (Hagigah 14a) discusses who is fit to be appointed a leader of the Jewish people. One opinion is that he needs to be fifty years old. Another opinion is that he needs to be proficient in the Five Books of Moshe.

We can bring a proof that we follow the second opinion. Shmuel passed away when he was fifty-two years old, and he was a ruler of the Jewish people for eleven years. Shmuel became a leader at the age of forty-one. Clearly one doesn't have to be over age fifty to become a leader.

At the time of the revolt, Korach was younger than fifty, as he was tasked in carrying the Ark. And the Levites no longer worked in the Tabernacle after the age of fifty. Korach thought to himself, *Just as my descendant Shmuel became a leader below the age of fifty, I too can become a leader even though I am not fifty.*

They confronted Moses together with two hundred and fifty men. (Bamidbar 16:2)

Why did Korach take two hundred and fifty men?

The tribe of Reuven lost their birthright. The double portion of land was given to the tribe of Yoseph, and the right to lead the

Jewish people was given to the tribe of Yehuda. Therefore, the tribes of Yoseph and Yehuda did not join the revolt together with Korach.

Each tribe had a Sanhedrin (judicial court) comprising of twenty-three judges. Each court also had two scribes to write the decisions for a total of twenty-five judges. There were ten remaining tribes: Twenty-five leaders from each tribe, giving us a total of two hundred and fifty men.

> *They confronted Moses together with two hundred and fifty men from the children of Israel, chieftains of the congregation, representatives of the assembly, men of repute.* (Bamidbar 16:2)

The Hebrew words *anshei shem* are generally translated as *men of repute*. However, the literal translation of *anshei shem* is *men of name*.

A question can be posed: How was Korach, together with these two hundred and fifty men, able to gather many of the Jewish people to rally around their cause to remove Moshe from his position of leadership? The Jewish people were well aware that Moshe had killed an Egyptian using the name of God and that he had performed many miracles.

The Midrash explains that these two hundred and fifty men were men of great stature; they were mature and wise. And they were given the secrets of God's name. That is why the Torah refers to them as *men of name*. The mistake people made was that since these two hundred and fifty men knew the secrets found in God's name, they would be considered on par with Moshe.

Chukat

Note: When God gave the Jewish people the Ten Commandments on Mount Sinai, after the Jewish people heard the first two commandments from God, they were unable to hear the rest because of the intense spiritual revelation that had occurred. They therefore asked Moshe to convey to them the rest of the commandments.

> *This is the statute of the Torah . . . You shall take a red heifer*
> (Bamidbar 19:2)

The Midrash on this verse, after quoting it, states, "This is what is written in the verse: *This is the Torah that Moshe placed before the Jewish people.*" (Devarim 4:44)

What is the link between this verse and the verse quoted in the Midrash?

The Midrash in Shir Hashirim (Song of Songs) states that each time God said one of the Ten Commandments, the evil inclination was uprooted from its place. And when the Jewish people said to Moshe, "You should speak to us and we will listen" (Shemot 20:16), the evil inclination was re-created.

Clearly, if God had said all the Ten Commandments, the evil inclination would have been destroyed forever. Then the Jewish people would not have sinned with the golden calf. The red heifer was an atonement for the golden calf.

We can now understand the Midrash. The reason the Jewish people had to bring a red heifer was an atonement for the golden calf. But why did the Jewish people have to bring a red heifer in the first place?

To answer this question, the Midrash quotes the verse, "This is the Torah that Moshe placed before the Jewish people." Because Moshe said some of the Ten Commandments, the evil inclination was re-created, which led the Jewish people to sin with the golden calf.[8]

---

8. *Midrash Yehonatan*

Note: The nation of Edom are descendants of Esau, the brother of Ya'akov. After the battle with the angel, Ya'akov's name was changed to Yisrael. The name Ya'akov can be translated to mean that he (Ya'akov) outwitted me (Esau). The name Yisrael means that he has reached a level of great stature.

This week's Torah reading discusses the various nations the Jewish people needed to traverse on their way to the Land of Israel.

> *Moshe sent messengers from Kadesh to the king of Edom: "So says your brother, Israel, 'You know of all the hardship that has befallen us.'"* (Bamidbar 20:14)

Why does Moshe not use the name Ya'akov and prefers to use the name Yisrael?

We learn from this verse a very important lesson in how one should conduct themselves. Generally speaking, when a person becomes very important or very wealthy, he forgets his friends and his family. Therefore, Moshe said your brother Yisrael. Even though Ya'akov had become a man of great stature, he did not forget that he has a brother called Esau.

Another reason Moshe used the name Yisrael and not Ya'akov: The verse says, "And he (Esau) said, 'Is it for this reason that he was named Ya'akov? For he has deceived me twice; he took my birthright, and behold, now he has taken my blessing.'" And he said, "Have you not reserved a blessing for me?"

Esau said that the reason my brother was called Ya'akov is because he outwitted me. Therefore, Moshe did not refer to Ya'akov by his more common name since he didn't want to remind the King of Edom what his ancestor Esau thought of Ya'akov and perhaps he would behave the same way with Moshe and the Jewish people in turn.

Balak

Note: The Hebrew word for numerous is rav. One of the great rabbis of the Talmudic era was a rabbi called Rav. Reb Yehonatan uses an opinion of Rav to explain the following verse. The rationale to do so is because this verse contains the name of the rabbi when it states that the people were numerous (rav).

> *Moab became terrified of the people, for they were numerous.*
> (Bamidbar 22:3)

In Devarim (2:9) the verse says, "*And the Lord said to me, 'Do not distress the Moabites.'*" If that is the case, why were the Moabites terrified of the Jewish people?

The Talmud (Gittin 38a) states that the nation Sichon stole land from the nation of Moab. As a result, the nations of Amon and Moab went to war against the nation of Sichon. Eventually, the Jewish people took the land from Sichon that they had stolen from Moab.

There is an argument in the Talmud (Sukkah 30b) whether one can steal someone else's property. Rav is of the opinion that you can, while Shmuel disagrees and says that land cannot be stolen. The law follows the opinion of Rav that land can be stolen.

We can now understand why "Moab were terrified of the Jewish people." Since the land of the Moabites had been taken by the Jewish people, the land will never be returned because "they were numerous (rav)" or the verse is saying, since we follow the opinion of Rav that land can be stolen.[9]

Note: Balak, the king of Moab, sought the assistance of Bilaam to help him defeat the Jewish people.

> *The Lord opened the mouth of the she-donkey, and she said to Bilaam, "What have I done to you that you have struck me these three times?"* (Bamidbar 22:28)

---

9. *Midrash Yehonatan*

The verse seems to imply that the donkey was always able to speak, and it simply needed to open its mouth and allow the words to be spoken.

The only other time in the Torah where an animal speaks to a human is when the snake spoke to Chava and convinced her to eat from the tree of knowledge. The verse states:

> Now the serpent was cunning, more than all the beasts of the field that the Lord God had made, and it said to the woman, "Did God indeed say, 'You shall not eat of any of the trees of the garden'?" (Bereishit 3:1)

This verse seems to imply that the snake was no different from any other creature except for the fact that it was more cunning. This seems to imply that all animals had the ability to communicate with mankind.

In truth, prior to the sin of Adam and Chava, the animals spoke like humans. The distinction between mankind and the animal kingdom was in the ability for mankind to comprehend the higher spiritual realms. Therefore, by the incident of the Bilaam and the donkey, God didn't have to create the ability for the donkey to speak—all animals had that ability. God simply had to open the mouth of the donkey and allow the donkey to communicate with Bilaam.

The Zohar explains the episode of the donkey and Bilaam: It wasn't that the donkey was speaking; rather, it was an angel whose name was *pi hatan* (mouth of the donkey) that spoke to Bilaam.

If it was an angel speaking, the angel must have been speaking *Lashon Hakodesh* (Hebrew) since angels do not know any other language. However, if it was the donkey speaking, it would have spoken in a language that Bilaam would have understood. Therefore, it would seem that it was the donkey speaking, since the purpose of the donkey speaking was to embarrass Bilaam in the presence of Balak's soldiers. If it was an angel speaking, Balak's soldiers did not understand Hebrew so Bilaam would not have been embarrassed.

Pinchas

Pinchas the son of Eliezer the son of Aaron the Cohen
(Bamidbar 25:11)

On the above verse, the Midrash states that it is appropriate for Pinchas to take his full reward. We need to understand what it means for "Pinchas to take his full reward."

The Talmud (Berachot 7a) states that there are four categories of Jewish people:

> *The tzaddik son of the tzaddik (righteous person).*
>
> *The tzaddik son of the rasha (wicked person).*
>
> *The rasha son of a tzaddik.*
>
> *The rasha son of the rasha.*

What is the distinction among these types of Jewish people in terms of their reward?

> *For the tzaddik son of the tzaddik, life is good.*
>
> *For the tzaddik son of the rasha, life is bad.*
>
> *For the rasha son of the tzaddik, life is good.*
>
> *For the rasha son of the rasha, life is bad.*

The Maharsha comments: It seems that the tzaddik son of a tzaddik and the rasha son of the tzaddik both receive the same reward: life is good for them. Similarly, the tzaddik son of the rasha and the rasha son of the rasha both receive the same reward: life is bad for them. That the tzaddik and the rasha receive the same reward seems somewhat difficult to comprehend.

The Maharsha explains that a person who is a tzaddik needs to leave his merit for his son since his son may be wicked and will not have merit in his own right. Therefore, the tzaddik son of the tzaddik and the rasha son of the tzaddik will both receive the same reward because they both inherit the merit of their fathers, who were both righteous. Likewise, the tzaddik son of the rasha and the rasha son of the rasha will similarly not inherit any merit because their fathers were wicked. And the tzaddik son of the rasha will not be rewarded for being a tzaddik as he needs to leave his merit for his own son.

If, however, the tzaddik son of a tzaddik knows that his own son will be a tzaddik (meaning the grandfather, father, and son are all righteous), there is no need for the father to leave his merit for his son, as his son will be rewarded in his own right as he is also a tzaddik.

The Talmud (Bava Batra 59a) quotes the verse in Kohelet 4:12: "a three stranded cord will not quickly be broken" and learns if a person is a tzaddik and his son is a tzaddik and his grandson is a tzaddik, one can be assured that his future generations will also be tzaddikim.

The verse said that Pinchas was the son of Elazar and the grandson of Aaron; all three were tzaddikim. Therefore, Pinchas knew that, based on the Talmud in Bava Batra, his descendants would be righteous. If so, Pinchas did not have to leave any of his merit for his son because his son would receive his reward on his own merit. Therefore, the Midrash states, "It is appropriate for Pinchas to take his full reward."

Note: There is a traditional Jewish superstition that a person who is born as a result of an illicit relationship will ultimately drown. Further, according to Torah law, a woman cannot marry her nephew.

Moshe and Elazar the Cohen spoke with them in the plains of Moab by the Jordan at Jericho, saying: (Bamidbar 26:3)

There were those who thought Moshe was born by an illegitimate union, as his father, Amram, was the nephew of his mother, Yocheved. It was not an illegitimate union as the prohibition of a woman marrying her nephew only became law *after* the giving of the Torah. Moshe, as a baby, was placed in the river, and God miraculously saved him. This proves that he was not born from an illegitimate union. If he had been, he should have drowned in the river. Likewise, Pharaoh believed that the Jewish women were forced to live with Egyptian men, and the children conceived were illegitimate. Therefore, the Jewish people passed through the Reed Sea to disprove this. Because if it was as Pharaoh thought, then they should have drowned in the sea instead of passing through the dry land.

Likewise, the nations believed that the Jewish people in the desert had not observed the laws of who was permitted to marry whom, and many illegitimate children were born. Therefore, God performed a miracle by splitting the Jordan River to prove that the Jewish children were all kosher. There really was no need for God to split the Jordan River. The river was not that wide and could have been crossed by boat.

Therefore, the Torah specifically mentions that Moshe and Elazar instructed the Jewish people by the Jordan River to be a testament that the Jewish people were all holy and pure.

Matot

Moshe spoke to the people, saying, "Arm from among you men for the army, that they can be against Midian, and carry out the revenge of the Lord against Midian. . . ." (Bamidbar 31:3)

Rashi writes that even though Moshe would pass away after going to war against Midian, he did it joyfully and without delay. How does Rashi know that Moshe carried out God's instruction with great joy and without delay?

Secondly, God instructed Moshe to tell the Jewish people that they should go to war against the Midianites to carry out the revenge of the Jewish people. Why then did Moshe, when instructing the Jewish people, change God's instruction and say they should go to war to seek God's revenge?

If Moshe would have conveyed God's instruction to the Jewish people as he had heard it, the Jewish people may have responded by saying, "We will forgo seeking our revenge against Midian and rather our leader Moshe remain alive."

Therefore, Moshe changed God's instruction to ensure the Jewish people would go immediately to war. This indicates that Moshe carried out his duty with great joy and without delay.

Masei

Note: The Torah reading lists the 42 times the Jewish people traveled and encamped during their sojourn in the desert.

These are the journeys (Bamidbar 33:1)

On this verse, the Midrash states that this section is proof that the positive commandment of saving life overrides the positive commandment of keeping Shabbat. Therefore, if someone is seriously ill, one must desecrate the Shabbat to save the person's life.

How is this section proof to the law brought in the Midrash?

The Talmud (Yevamot 71a) says that the Jewish people did not circumcise their sons while they were in the desert. Two possible reasons are given: either because the challenges of travel interfered with their ability to circumcise their sons or because a northerly wind blew in the desert, and it is considered dangerous for a northerly wind to blow on a circumcised child.

In this section, it says the Jewish people traveled and encamped. If the reason they didn't circumcise their sons was due to the challenges of travel, they should have circumcised their sons while they were encamped. Therefore, we must say that the true reason is because of the dangers of the northerly wind. They could not circumcise their sons even when they were encamped because the northerly wind, which blew whether they traveled or encamped, would be dangerous for a newly circumcised boy.

This proves that the positive commandment of saving life takes precedence over the positive commandment of circumcision. The positive commandment of circumcision overrides the laws of Shabbat therefore, an eight day old boy can be circumcised on Shabbat. Saving a life overrides circumcision. Circumcision overrides Shabbat. By extension, saving life will therefore definitely override the laws of Shabbat. Hence, the midrash states that this section is proof that the positive commandment of saving life overrides the obligation of keeping Shabbat.

Note: The tribes of Reuven and Gad wanted to remain in the Transjordan and not enter the Land of Israel proper. Moshe consented to their request; however, he instructed that half the tribe of Menashe would join them. Ephraim and Menashe were the two sons of Yoseph. Yehoshua was from the tribe of Ephraim.

Moshe gave the descendants of Gad and the descendants of Reuven and half the tribe of Menashe the kingdom of Sichon,
(Bamidbar 32:33)

The tribes of Reuven and Gad wanted to remain in the Transjordan. Why did Moshe say that half the tribe of Menashe would join them?

The tribe of Reuven joined with Korach in his revolt against Moshe. Moshe felt that the tribe of Reuven wanted to remain in the Transjordan because they did not want to accept the rulership of Yehoshua. Therefore, Moshe added half the tribe of Menashe. Yehoshua was from the tribe of Ephraim, and Moshe felt that the tribe of Menashe would not revolt against Yehoshua.

Why did Moshe send only half the tribe of Menashe?

Ya'akov had stated in Bereishit 48:5:

Ephraim and Menashe shall be mine like Reuven and Shimon.

This means the tribes of Menashe and Ephraim would have the same legal status as the tribes of Reuven and Shimon.

The phrase "Ephraim *and* Menashe" can be understood to mean "Ephraim *or* Menashe." This would mean that Ephraim or Menashe would be equal to both Reuven and Shimon.

Since Moshe was only concerned that the tribe of Reuven would revolt, he only needed half the tribe of Menashe to counterbalance the tribe of Reuven if they were to revolt against Yehoshua.

Devarim

These are the words that Moshe spoke to all of Israel
(Devarim 1:1)

WHY DOES THE VERSE SAY THAT MOSHE SPOKE to *all* of Israel?
It would have been sufficient for the verse to say that Moshe spoke to
the Jewish people.

The Talmud (Moed Katan 21a) states that this section was spoken
three days after the passing of Aaron. As such, Moshe was in *aveilut*
(mourning) and prohibited from teaching Torah. How then could
Moshe be teaching the Jewish people? The Talmud answers: If the
masses need a person to teach them Torah, the person is permitted.
Therefore, Moshe was permitted to teach Torah even though he was
in mourning.

Therefore, the verse states that Moshe spoke to *all* of Israel. Since
he was teaching all of Israel, he was permitted to do so.

These are the words that Moshe spoke to all of Israel
(Devarim 1:1)

Rashi writes that Moshe rebuked the Jewish people. He first
rebuked them for the revolt of Korach and then he rebuked them for
the sin of the golden calf. The question can be asked: if the episode of
the golden calf occurred prior to the episode of Korach's revolt, why
did Moshe rebuke them for Korach's revolt first?

The Jewish people may have had a justification and a response to
the sin of the golden calf. They could have said God gave the Torah
to Moshe and He didn't give it to us. Therefore, we did not sin by the
golden calf.

By the revolt of Korach, one of the claims Korach made was that
we are all holy people because we all heard on Mount Sinai the command, "I am the Lord your God."

If, in fact, all the Jewish people heard the commandment not to serve idols, they no longer could argue that the prohibition against idol worship was only given to Moshe. Therefore, Moshe first rebuked them for Korach's revolt, and once he did that, he could now rebuke them for the episode of the golden calf.

Va'etchanan

I entreated the Lord (Devarim 3:23)

The rabbis tell us that Moshe prayed 515 times to be allowed to enter the Land of Israel. This is seen in the fact that the Hebrew word for *entreated* is *vaetchanan*, which has the numerical value of 515. Besides the fact that this word has a numerical value of 515, we can deduce that Moshe prayed 515 times from the following:

The Midrash says, on the 15th of Av, Moshe pleaded with God and asked, "Let me pass over and see the Land of Israel."

The Talmud tells us that on the 15th of Av, the Jewish people stopped dying in the desert, and Moshe thought perhaps he too would not pass away in the desert. From the 15th of Av till the 7th of Adar, the day Moshe passed away, is 200 days. There are twenty-eight Shabbatot during this period of time, which need to be removed from the calculation since one cannot ask for personal needs on Shabbat. We are left with 172 days.

We pray three times a day giving 516 *tefilot* (prayers). The Jewish people stopped dying in the morning so on the evening of the 15th, Moshe did not pray to be allowed into Israel. We therefore take away one prayer, leaving us with 515 prayers. This is the basis for how we know that Moshe prayed 515 times.

During the period between 15th of Av and the 7th of Adar, there are the festivals of Rosh Hashanah, Yom Kippur, and Sukkot when one is not permitted to ask for personal requests. Thus, we would have fewer than 515 prayers. Moshe passed away on the 7th of Adar. That year, the 7th of Adar fell on Shabbat. If the 7th of Adar was on Shabbat, then Rosh Hashanah and Sukkot of that year also fell on Shabbat.

Teach them thoroughly to your sons. (Devarim 6:7)

The Hebrew word for *teach them* is *v'shinantom*. The Talmud states that we should read the word *v'shinantom* as if it was written *v'shilashtom*, meaning that one should divide one's day in terms of learning into three parts: one-third to the study of *chumash*, one-third to *Mishnah*, and one-third to the Talmud.

Why is this so?

If one would only study *chumash*, he would not be able to fulfill the commandments properly. For example, the mitzvah of wearing tefillin: If we only had the written Torah, a person would not know how many sections of the Torah should be placed in the boxes of the tefillin. Therefore, we need the *Mishnah* to teach us that four sections of the Torah must be placed in each box.

If we would only have the *Mishnah*, one would think there is no link between the written Torah and the oral tradition. We therefore need the Talmud, as it is the bridge that links the two.

Using *tefillin* as an example, the Torah doesn't say how many sections are placed in each box. The Mishnah says four. What is the basis for the Mishnah's ruling?

The Talmud explains that the Torah, when discussing the commandment of Tefillin, refers to the *tefillin* worn on one's head as *totafos*, and the Talmud explains the word *totafos* is really two words joined together: *tot* and *fos*. *Tot* in Coptic means *two* and *fos* in Phrygian means *two*. We now have an understanding why tefillin has four sections—thereby linking the written and oral tradition.

The Torah said *v'shinantom*, to learn diligently. The only way one can learn diligently and fully comprehend it is by *v'shilashtom*, by dividing one's learning into three parts: Chumash, Mishna, and Talmud.

Eikev

Note: The Ten Commandments were engraved into the tablets. The Talmud states that the letters mem *and* samech *were written in a miraculous manner, as both letters had a floating piece in the middle.*

I grasped the two tablets, cast them out of my two hands, and shattered them before your eyes. (Devarim 9:17)

Rashi explains that the two tablets were the same. What does Rashi mean by this?

The Talmud (Shekalim 16b) brings forth an argument: Were the Ten Commandments written on each tablet or were the first five commandments written on the first tablet and the last five commandments written on the second tablet?

The commentaries ask: How was Moshe able to break the tablets? The tablets were made from a material called *sanpurin,* which is unbreakable. They answer that the actual tablets did not shatter. Rather, the floating part in the letters *mem* and *samech* fell away, and that is what is meant when the Torah said that Moshe shattered the tablets.

The letters *mem* and *samech* are found only in the first five commandments. If we accept the opinion that each tablet had only five commandments written on it, then the second tablet should not have shattered because the second tablet had no letter *mem* or letter *samech.* Therefore, the Ten Commandments were written on each of the two tablets, and both tablets shattered.

We now understand Rashi when he said the two tablets were the same: On each tablet was written the Ten Commandments.

Note: Many times, the Torah will use the word et. The word et has no translation. It is used as a preposition to introduce a direct object.

You shall fear God (Devarim 10:20)

The Talmud (Pesachim 22b) writes that Shimon Hoamusni explained that each time the Torah uses the word *et*, it is coming to teach us a new law, and he went through the whole Torah explaining each time *et* is written what new law is being taught. When he came to the verse that reads, *et Hashem Elokeicha tirah* (You shall fear God), he desisted—as he said it was impossible to extend the fear of God to anything else.

Rabbi Akiva said that the word *et* in the verse comes to include the Torah scholar—that a person is obligated to fear a Torah scholar.

Why didn't Shimon Hoamusni learn, as Rabbi Akiva did, that the verse comes to include the Torah scholar?

In truth, there should be no need for the Torah to teach that one must have respect for and fear the Torah scholar since the world exists because of the Torah and in order for the Jewish people to study Torah. Therefore, Shimon Hoamusni felt that the word *et* in this verse wasn't needed to teach us this law—it is a given that one must fear the Torah scholar.

Rabbi Akiva, on the other hand, was initially an unlearned individual, and the Talmud (Pesachim 49b) records that when Rabbi Akiva was unlearned, he once said something derogatory about Torah scholars. Therefore, based on his life experiences and his understanding of the attitudes of the unlearned, Rabbi Akiva felt a person would not fear the Torah scholar without being instructed. He therefore needed the *et* in this verse to teach us this.

Note: The Talmud states that whenever the Torah uses the word v'haya, it means it is a moment of joy and happiness.

> *It will be if you will surely listen to my commandments . . .*
> *to love God your God (Devarim 11:13)*

It would seem that the words "it will be" are superfluous.

The Talmud (Bava Metzia 85b) asks why God destroyed the First Temple. The Talmud responds, because the Jewish people did not make the appropriate blessing prior to the study of Torah. At that time, the Jewish people had transgressed many of God's commandments. Why then does the Talmud single out not saying a blessing prior to learning Torah as the reason for the destruction of the Temple?

The Talmud, in its answer, is alluding to the fact that when the Jewish people were observing the commandments, they did not fulfill them with a sense of joy and happiness. That is why we have remained in exile so long.

When God created mankind, he created him for his own benefit. God did not create mankind for God's own pleasure. Rather, God created man so that he should fulfill God's commandments and be rewarded for it. If, however, man doesn't fulfill the commandments with happiness, it is as if man is doing them begrudgingly for the sake of God, which goes against the very purpose for man's creation.

We will now understand why the word *v'haya* means that "it will be" is not superfluous. "It will be" (if you serve God with joy) and listen to His commandments . . . you will be rewarded accordingly. The manner you fulfill the commandments is crucial.

Re'eh

Note: Three times a year, every Jewish male had to make a pilgrimage to the Temple in Jerusalem.

And it will be the place the Lord your God will choose in which to establish His Name there you shall bring all that I am commanding you (Devarim 12:11)

And He will give you rest from all your enemies surrounding you, and you will dwell securely. (Devarim 12:10)

The Jewish people were obligated to build the Temple only after they had defeated the enemy and settled in the Land of Israel. Why was this so?

Going up to Jerusalem three times a year was not easy. They had to travel great distances and leave behind their homes and fields. God had promised the Jewish people that while they were traveling back and forth to Jerusalem, they would be protected. The Talmud states that someone traveling to fulfill God's commandment will not be harmed. However, this rule applies only if one is traveling in a safe place. If the area is unsafe, a person will not be protected even though they are doing a mitzvah.

Prior to conquering and settling the land, Israel was not a safe place. If they would have immediately built the Temple, they would have been unable to travel to Jerusalem three times a year. Therefore, the Temple was built only once the Land of Israel was conquered and settled and was a safe place.

That will explain the order of the verses. Initially, the Torah says, "you will dwell securely," and then the Torah says, "the place the Lord your God will choose in which to establish His Name."

You shall tithe (Devarim 14:22)

Note: The Hebrew for "you shall tithe" is aseh t'aseh. *The Hebrew word* t'aseh *can also mean "wealth."*

The Midrash quotes the verse "then you shall rejoice with all the good" (Devarim 26:11) and says, true goodness is the Torah. Therefore, Moshe warned the Jewish people, "You shall tithe." What is the connection between the Torah being good and Moshe instructing the Jewish people to give tithe?

Concerning the greatness of Torah, in Mishlei (Proverbs) 3:16, it is written:

Length of days in its right hand; in its left hand are riches and honor.

The commentaries explain that if someone learns Torah with the correct intention, he will be rewarded with *length of days* (long life); if a person learns Torah with incorrect intention, he will be rewarded *with riches and honor*.

The Maharsha asks, if a person learns Torah for the right reasons and is blessed only with long life and not with riches and honor, how will he survive? He will be poor, and the Talmud says a poor person is considered a dead person. How then will he have long life?

The Maharsha therefore explains the verse in Mishlei to mean that if a person learns Torah for the right reason, he will be blessed with both long life and riches. If the person studies Torah for the wrong reason, he will be blessed only with riches.

The Talmud also says that since the verse reads *aseh t'aseh*, we learn that if one gives tithe, he will become wealthy.

We will now understand the Midrash quoted above: "with all the good, true goodness is the Torah." If a person studies Torah with the right intention, he will be blessed with both long life and wealth (according to the Maharsha). Being that he has become wealthy, he may have no interest in giving tithe since the incentive of giving tithe as a means to become wealthy is no longer an incentive; he is wealthy anyway. Therefore, Moshe warned the Jewish people, "You shall tithe" whether or not you are already wealthy.

Shoftim

Note: According to Biblical law, only sons inherit their father's property. If a person only has daughters, they will inherit their father's property. However, when the daughters marry, the property is transferred to their husbands. If the husband is from another tribe, then the land will be transferred to another tribe. Zelophehad was from the tribe of Yoseph.

> *When you come to the land . . . I will set a king over myself.*
> (Devarim 17:14)

It seems that Rambam's opinion is that the Jewish people were obligated to appoint a king only after they had conquered and divided the Land of Israel. Why couldn't they appoint a king while they were still in the desert?

At the end of Bamidbar, the Torah states:

> *And our master was commanded by the Lord to give the inheritance of Zelophehad our brother to his daughters. Now, if they marry a member of another tribe of the children of Israel, their inheritance will be diminished from the inheritance of our father, and it will be added to the inheritance of the tribe into which they marry* (Bamidbar 36:2–3)

Their complaint was that if Zelophehad's property would go to his daughters when they married, the land would be transferred to other tribes. The question can be asked, Why were the brothers of Zelophehad so upset? Just as they would lose land because their brother's daughters may marry men from another tribe, there will be times when men from the tribe of Yoseph will marry women who will bring into their marriage property that will be transferred to the tribe of Yoseph.

The brothers were not upset about the transfer of land from one tribe to another. Such transfers will happen all the time. They were upset specifically about *their* brother's land going to another tribe. Zelophehad's land was given to his daughters as a direct instruction by God as the verse says, "our master was commanded by the Lord to give the inheritance of Zelophehad our brother to his daughters." Land designated by God should always remain within the tribe.

The law is that when a king would go to war, he would divide the spoils between himself and his soldiers. He would take half and the soldiers would receive the other half. If the king had been appointed while the Jewish people were still in the desert, half of any land they would have conquered when they entered Israel would belong to the king.

The Land of Israel was divided among the tribes according to God's instructions. The Jewish people (as Zelophehad's brothers were) would have been upset if half of the land designated by God went to another tribe. That is why the king was appointed only after they entered the Land of Israel.

Note: The Cohanim and the Levites did not receive land in Israel; rather, they were supported by the various dues that the Jewish people were obligated to give.

> *This shall be the Cohanim's due, from the people, from those who perform a slaughter, be it an ox or a sheep, he shall give the Cohen the foreleg, the jaws and the maw (Devarim 18:3)*

The tribe of Levi were not involved in the two sins symbolized by the ox and the sheep.

When the Jewish people came to the Reed Sea, they didn't know what to do. There was a segment of the Jewish people who wanted to return to Egypt. The god of the Egyptians was the sheep. The tribe of Levi did not want to return to Egypt. The tribe of Levi did not dance around the golden calf.

When the verse said, "Be it an ox or sheep," the verse is explaining why the tribe of Levi was entitled to the various gifts—since they did not sin with the sheep or with the ox. As a result, they merited to receive the foreleg, the jaw, and the maw. Why specifically these three parts of the animal?

The leg because Moshe broke the tablets with his hands, thereby saving the Jewish people from annihilation.

The jaw because of all the prayers Moshe prayed to save the Jewish people.

The maw due to the fact that Moshe fasted when he was in heaven receiving the Torah.

Ki Teitzei

You shall send away the mother bird and you shall take the offspring for yourself (Devarim 22:7)

Seemingly, the verse could have been written, "You shall take the offspring." Why was it necessary to add the words *for yourself*?

The Midrash states that the reward for fulfilling the commandment of sending away the mother bird is, if one wasn't blessed with children, one would be blessed with children. This is alluded to in the verse: "You shall send away the mother bird," and the reward for fulfilling this mitzvah is "take the offspring"; you will be blessed with children "for yourself"; The words *for yourself* are no longer unnecessary.[10]

And you shall keep a stake in addition to your weapons; and it shall be, when you sit down outside (to relieve yourself) you shall dig with it, and you shall return and cover your excrement (Devarim 23:14)

Why was it necessary to cover the excrement?

If the Jewish people would not have sinned, they would have always eaten the *manna* (food that fell from heaven). The *manna* is the food eaten by the angels. When the Jewish people ate the *manna* in the desert, they did not have to relieve themselves. The *manna* had no wastage; all the *manna* was absorbed by the body. By having to relieve themselves, the Jewish people were displaying that they had sinned. Therefore, they were obligated to cover the excrement.

Another reason given is that the Jewish people sinned by the idol Peor. The service of the idol Peor was to bow to the excrement. When a person wants to do *teshuvah* (repent), he needs to go to the other

---

10. *Midrash Yehonatan*

extreme. Therefore, we cover all excrement in order we should not even see it.

Fathers shall not be put to death because of sons
(Devarim 24:16)

Note: An Ir HaNidachat is a city in Israel in which the majority of its citizens are idolaters. The Torah says, such a city's inhabitants must be put to death and all the citizens possessions need to be destroyed.

The Midrash states that an Ir HaNidachat can be turned into gardens or orchards. Aba Chanan says that one cannot turn an Ir HaNidachat into gardens or orchards because the verse says, "Fathers shall not be put to death because of sons." The verse is speaking about the testimony of the sons against their father.

What is the connection between an Ir HaNidachat and the testimony of the sons?

The Talmud (Bava Kamma 88a) states that the verse "Fathers shall not be put to death because of sons" isn't coming to teach us that a father will not die because of his sons' sins since this law is clearly stated in the second half of the verse that says, "Each man will be put to death for his own transgression." Rather the phrase, "Fathers shall not be put to death because of sons" is teaching us that we do not accept the testimony of sons who testify that their father should receive the death penalty.

A question can be posed: Why do we need the verse "Fathers shall not be put to death because of sons" to teach us that we do not accept the testimony of sons who testify that their father should receive the death penalty. Even without the verse, we would know that we don't accept the testimony of the sons.

The law is that we don't accept testimony from witnesses if they will benefit from their testimony. If we accept the testimony of the sons that their father should be put to death, the sons in turn will inherit their father's estate. Therefore, we don't need the verse.

To resolve this question, we must say the verse is speaking of a case where the father is living in an Ir HaNidachat, and all of the father's assets will be destroyed and the sons will not have any financial gain by testifying against their father. Therefore, we need the verse to teach us that, even in such a case, sons cannot testify against their fathers.

If, however, we follow the opinion that we can turn an Ir HaNidachat into gardens, then our assumption that we don't accept testimony from witnesses who will gain financially from their testimony remains. We therefore must say that we will follow the opinion that we cannot turn an Ir HaNidachat into gardens.

We will now be able to understand the connection the Midrash makes between an Ir HaNidachat not becoming a garden and the verse, "Fathers shall not be put to death because of sons."

Aba Chanan says that one cannot turn an Ir HaNidachat into gardens or orchards. The reason being the verse says, "Fathers shall not be put to death because of sons." The verse is speaking about the testimony of the sons (against their father).

Only in a case where the witnesses (the sons) have no financial benefit (the father lives in an Ir HaNidachat and we follow the opinion of Aba Chanan that an Ir HaNidachat cannot be turned into a garden) will we need the verse, "Fathers shall not be put to death because of sons." The verse is speaking about the testimony of the sons (against their father), and there is no financial benefit in their testimony (since an Ir HaNidachat can't be turned into a garden).

Ki Tavo

Note: A farmer in the Land of Israel was obligated to bring the first fruit (bikkurim) up to the Temple and a special prayer was recited.

The Shemoneh Esrei is a section of the daily prayers. The congregation first says this prayer quietly to themselves and then the person leading the service repeats it aloud. During the repetition, the congregation answers *amen* after each blessing and also says in unison the prayer called Kedushah. If one is saying the silent Shemoneh Esrei and the person leading the service begins the repetition, the person still in his silent Shemoneh Esrei cannot answer *amen* or say Kedushah with the congregation.

> *And you shall call out and say before the Lord, your God, "An Aramean sought to destroy my forefather."* (Devarim 26:5)

The Midrash on this verse asks: If a person is leading the service, can he answer *amen* after the priestly blessing? The Midrash answers that he should not because this may make him confused, and he will not know where to continue in the priestly blessing.

What is the connection between the verse that discusses bringing the bikkurim and the priestly blessings?

The Talmud (Berachot 34a) brings the same law as quoted in the Midrash. Tosafot asks: Why does the Talmud explain the prohibition of the person leading the prayers from answering *amen* during the priestly benediction because he may become confused? The Talmud could have answered that *amen* can't be answered because answering *amen* is an interruption in the prayers, and one is prohibited from interrupting the prayers by adding words. Tosafot says that the word *amen* is not considered an interruption.

Rashi on the Talmud (Sukkah 38b) writes that if one is praying the silent Shemoneh Esrei and the congregation is saying *amen* or

Kedushah, he should stop praying and listen as the congregation says amen or Kedushah. And, by listening, it will be considered as if he is reciting what the congregation is saying.

Tosafot (Sukkah 38b) notes that the Talmud (Berachot 21b) states that if someone comes late to the synagogue and the congregation is already saying the silent Shemoneh Esrei, he should first answer Kedushah and then he should begin saying his Shemoneh Esrei.

Tosafot asks why, according to Rashi, is there a need to wait? The person should begin his Shemoneh Esrei, and when the congregation reaches Kedushah, he should remain silent and listen as the congregation answers Kedushah? This would seem to imply that even remaining silent and just listening is considered an interruption.

Tosafot answers: In truth, remaining silent is not deemed an interruption; rather, it is preferable to actually say the words (that is why the Talmud in Berachot said to wait to answer with the congregation) and listening to the congregation say the words. However, if one did hear the congregation say the words, one would have fulfilled one's obligation.

What source states that saying the words is better than simply hearing the words from someone else? The Mishnah (Bikkurim) states that if someone knows how to read Hebrew, he was given the text of what needed to be read when bringing the first fruit. If he didn't know how to read, someone would read the text, and the person bringing the fruit would repeat after him. People were embarrassed to have it become known that they didn't know how to read; they therefore instituted that everyone would hear the text and then repeat the words.

The Midrash states that it is alluded to in the Torah that the text needs to be read to the person bringing the fruit and then he repeats the words as the verse says, "You shall answer and you shall say"—meaning you shall respond and you shall say what you have just heard.

Why was it necessary for the person to actually repeat the words aloud? Why isn't it sufficient to simply hear someone else say the words?

The above Mishna and Midrash are proof that the mitzvah is far greater to actually say the words oneself than to hear them from someone else.

We will now understand the connection of bringing the bikkurim to the law whether the *chazzan* can answer *amen*.

Once we have established that it is better to actually say the words than listen to someone else say them, I might have thought that the chazzan should answer *amen* himself (and not rely on simply hearing it form the congregation); therefore, the Talmud says the reason you don't answer *amen* is because it could cause the chazzan to forget where he is up to in his prayers.

You shall be blessed in the city and you shall be blessed
in the field (Devarim 28:3)

Only the Jewish people who came to receive the priestly blessing were blessed; if, however, someone intentionally remained in the field, they did not receive the priestly blessing.

However, when God blesses the Jewish people, even the Jewish people who remain in the field are also blessed. Therefore, the verse says, "you shall be blessed in the field." The previous verse says, "You will receive all these blessings." Why does the verse include the word *all*? It would seem redundant.

Ya'akov was a man of the city, and Esau was a man of the field. Yitzchak blessed them accordingly. The verse said "all these blessings" to include the blessing given to Esau, which were in turn given to the Jewish people. Therefore, the verse said, "you shall be blessed in the field"—meaning the blessing given to Esau, who was a man of the field, will also be given to the Jewish people.

Nitzavim

Even if your exiles are at the end of the heavens, the Lord, your
God, will gather you from there, and He will take you from there.
(Devarim 30:4)

How are we to understand the phrase "at the ends of the heavens"? If
someone is a tzaddik, they are considered close to heaven. If he sins,
then he distances himself from heaven. If he sins more, he distances
himself more—until it reaches a point when the person is considered
at the end of heaven.

Even a Jew who is so distant, God will gather them in the Messianic era.

Vayelech

He said to them, "Today I am one hundred and twenty years old. I can no longer go or come, and the Lord said to me, 'You shall not cross the Jordan'" (Devarim 31:2)

Rashi explains that Moshe was saying, "On this day I was born and on this day I will die." Another explanation given for "I can no longer go or come" means the channels of transmission and the wellsprings of wisdom were closed up from him.

The verse in Shemot 23:26 says, "I will fill the number of your days." The Talmud (Sotah 13a) states that the verse means that the righteous will pass away on the day they are born.

The Maharsha asks, "If the verse means that God will complete the years of the righteous, then if someone is born on the fifth day of Tishrei, then he should pass away a day earlier on the fourth day of Tishrei, thereby completing the year. If, however, he passes away on the fifth of Tishrei, then he has entered the first day of his next year?"

The Maharsha answers by quoting the verse in Tehillim (Psalms) that a person's life will be seventy years. And concerning a person who lives seventy years, the Torah said, "I will fill the number of your days." The Hebrew word for *fill* is *emaleh*, which has a numerical value of seventy-one—meaning a righteous person who lives for seventy years will pass away on his birthday. Thus, he would have entered his seventy-first year. And the Talmud says, "One day in the new year is like a complete year." The righteous person will have had a filled life; he will have lived seventy-one years.

The question posed by the Maharsha can be asked on Moshe. Moshe said he would pass away on the day he was born; if that was the case, he would have lived an extra day, taking him into his 121st year, and if a day is like a year, he will have lived 121 years. (The Maharsha answer is not applicable to Moshe as the Maharsha was discussing a situation in which a person lives seventy years.)

There is an argument over which day of the week Moshe passed away on. One opinion is that he died on Shabbat; the second opinion is that he died the day before, on Friday.

The Maharsha (Hagigah 5b) compares death to someone who is without Torah.

We will now be able to understand the two commentaries of Rashi and whether Moshe passed away on Friday or Shabbat. Moshe was born on the 7th of Adar, and he passed away on the 7th of Adar on Shabbat. However, on the Friday, Moshe's wellsprings of wisdom closed, and since Moshe was without Torah, it is as if he passed away on Friday. Therefore, Moshe's years were complete: He was born on the 7th of Adar and passed away on the 6th of Adar. A day later, on Shabbat, the 7th of Adar, his soul departed from his body.

And God said to me, "You will not cross the Jordan (river)
The Lord your God He will cross before you . . . Yehoshua
he will cross before you." (Devarim 31:3)

The verse seems to contradict itself. Initially, it says God will cross before you; then it says Yehoshua will cross before you. Also, why did Moshe request to enter the Land of Israel when Yehoshua had already been appointed, and if Moshe would have remained alive and entered the Land of Israel, there would have been two leaders, and we know there can only be one ruler of the Jewish people at any given time.

In the Messianic era, there will be two leaders: Moshiach (the son of Yoseph) and Moshiach (the son of David). Moshiach (the son of Yoseph) will lead the Jewish people in its battles against their enemies, while Moshiach (the son of David) will teach the Jewish people Torah.

Moshe thought that he could enter the land together with Yehoshua. Yehoshua would lead the Jewish people in its battles against its enemies, while he, Moshe, would teach the Jewish people Torah. Therefore, the verse says that God will cross the Jordan—meaning that God would lead the Jewish people in battle and Yehoshua would cross over and he would teach the Jewish people Torah. Therefore, there would be no need for Moshe to cross over as well.

Note: At the conclusion of the sabbatical year when the farmers would leave their fields fallow, all the Jewish people were obligated to go to Jerusalem and hear the king read sections of the Torah. This commandment was known as Hakhel.

> *Moshe commanded them saying, at the end of seven years*
> *at an appointed time. (Devarim 31:10)*

God instituted the law of Shemitah (the sabbatical year) because, during the previous six years, the farmer was preoccupied with working the land and it was difficult for him to find time to study Torah. Therefore, God said, "Every seventh year, you will not work and you will be able to dedicate yourself to the study of Torah."

At the conclusion of Shemitah, a person may have thought that he had studied enough during the past year. Therefore, the Torah gives us the mitzvah of Hakhel—when we must all once again go and study Torah.

Ha'azinu

My lesson will drip like rain; my word will flow like dew
(Devarim 32:2)

The word *rain* refers to the tzaddikim of each generation who are few in number. They are compared to rain; just as rain doesn't fall all the time, likewise tzaddikim are few in number.

The word *dew* refers to the average person. Just as dew is constantly found, the average person is always present.

Vzot HaBracha

Note: The word reishit *means the first.*

And there was no other prophet who arose in Israel like Moshe
(Devarim 34:10)

The Midrash states that Kohelet (King Solomon) wanted to be like
Moshe, and a heavenly voice said, "and properly recorded words of
truth" there will be no prophet like Moshe.

The Midrash offers two reasons the Torah began with the word
reishit: Either because Moshe is called *reishit* or because the conclud-
ing letters of the opening three words—*breishit bare Elokim*—spells the
word *emet*, meaning truth.

The following question can be posed: Why is the word *emet* not
written in its correct order? Rather, in the first three words, the word
tof is written first and then the *aleph* and then the *mem*. We must say
that the word *emet* is alluded to in the three words that come after the
word *Bereishit*. The words being *bare elokim et*, which spells the word
emet in its correct order.

This being the case, why did the Torah begin with the word *Bereishit* since we don't learn anything from it?

While we do not use the word *Bereishit* to spell the word *emet*, we
do use the word *Bereishit* to teach us that the world was created in the
merit of Moshe. That being the case, there will never be a prophet like
Moshe.

PART TWO

Shabbat, the Yomim Tovim, the Beit Hamikdash, Galut, and the End of Days

Shabbat

Why Do We Keep Shabbat?

Note: When the Jewish people left Egypt, the Erev Rav (the mixed multitude of other nations) joined the Jewish people and left with them. It was the mixed multitude who convinced the Jewish people to worship the golden calf. The first set of tablets were broken because the Jewish people served the golden calf. The second set of tablets were given to the Jewish people some three months later.

IN THE FIRST SET OF TABLETS, the reason given for observing Shabbat was to remind us that God created the world in six days and rested on the seventh. In the second set of tablets, the reason given for observing Shabbat was to remind us that we were enslaved in Egypt and God took us out of Egypt.

Shabbat as a reminder of creation was applicable to the non-Jewish people who left Egypt together with the Jewish people. However, once these non-Jewish people were the cause for the golden calf, God no longer wanted to include them in the second set of tablets. Therefore, in the second set of tablets, the reason given for observing Shabbat was to remind us that we were once enslaved in Egypt. This reason does not apply to the mixed multitude because they were not enslaved in Egypt.

Shabbat Atones

The obligation to keep Shabbat is mentioned prior to the laws of building the *Mishkan* (Tabernacle). The Mishkan was an atonement for the sin of the golden calf. However, building the Mishkan was not sufficient to be considered a complete atonement. The Jewish people also needed to observe the Shabbat to be fully absolved of the sin of the golden calf. As the Talmud (Shabbat 118b) states, "Whoever observes the Shabbat properly, even if he is an idol worshipper, his sins are forgiven." Therefore, the obligation to keep Shabbat is mentioned prior to building the Mishkan. To impress upon us only through the observance of the Shabbat and the Mishkan will the Jewish people be forgiven for the sin of the golden calf.[11]

Cutting the Fingernails

The custom is that one should cut their fingernails on the eve of Shabbat. Why is this so? The fingernails extend beyond a person's fingers. The nails symbolize the desire to take that which doesn't belong to the person and desire that which isn't his. The eve of Shabbat is an opportune time to do *teshuva* (repent). By cutting the fingernails, the person is saying he will not take or even desire what is not his.[12]

Kiddush

When a person makes Kiddush on Friday night, he is rectifying Adam's sin of eating from the tree of knowledge. The Talmud (Berachot 40a) records an argument: What fruit did Adam eat? One opinion was that he ate wheat; the other opinion was that he ate grapes. Therefore, there is also an argument recorded in the Talmud on what a person should make Kiddush on Friday night. One opinion says on a cup of wine, since Adam's sin was eating grapes. The other opinion is he should make Kiddush on the two loaves of challah since Adam's sin was eating wheat.

---

11. *Tiferet Yehonatan*
12. *Yaaroth Devash*

Cutting the Challah

Adam sinned when he ate from the Tree of Knowledge. The tree of knowledge contained within it elements of good and elements of evil. That is why we cut the challah into two pieces: to indicate the good and evil in the tree of knowledge. The sin of Adam was forgiven by the festival of Shavuot when we celebrate the giving of the Torah to the Jewish people. Therefore, on Shavuot, we bring two *complete* loaves of challah as a sacrifice, indicating that there is no more evil in the world.

Three Meals

A person who eats three meals on Shabbat is considered to have great faith in God. Why is this so? A person's nature is that the more they make, the more they are willing to spend on personal needs. On Shabbat, a person is not allowed to work. There is no income on Shabbat. One would imagine that, on Shabbat, a person would not want to overspend because there is no money coming in.

A person normally has two meals a day. The law is that on Shabbat a person is obligated to have three meals, one meal more than normal. Therefore, if a person eats three meals on Shabbat, he is demonstrating his faith in God that God will provide for all his needs.

Lighting a Fire

The Torah states:

You shall not light a fire in any of your dwelling places on the Shabbat day. (Shemot 35:3)

There are thirty-nine prohibitions on Shabbat. One of the prohibitions is that one may not light a fire on Shabbat. Why does the Torah specifically mention the prohibition of lighting a fire but does not mention any of the other prohibitions?

The first set of tablets states that the reason we observe the Shabbat is to remind us that God created the world in six days and rested on the seventh. A person is prohibited on Shabbat from those actions that God used in creating the world during the first six days.

The Talmud (Pesachim 54a) states that fire was created on Motzei Shabbat (Saturday night). If that is the case, one may have assumed one could light a fire on the Shabbat, since fire was not used in the creation of the world. Therefore, the Torah had to specifically mention the prohibition of lighting a fire on the Shabbat.[13]

Day of Rest

Note: Moshe destroyed the first set of tablets because the Jewish people were dancing around the golden calf. The second set of tablets were given to the Jewish people via Moshe a number of months later on Yom Kippur. There are a number of differences in the language used in the first set in comparison to the second set.

In the second set, when discussing the obligation to keep Shabbat, the Torah states:

> *In order that your male servant and your maidservant may rest like you. (Devarim 5:14)*

Why is this mentioned specifically in the second set and not in the first set? Rashi writes, if it would not be for Shabbat, man would work without rest. Therefore, God chose Shabbat to be a day of rest. One may have assumed that if the Jewish people had rested during the course of the week, they would no longer be obligated to rest on the coming Shabbat—for example, the Shabbat following Yom Kippur. Since one is not permitted to work on Yom Kippur, one may have come to the conclusion that since the Jewish people rested during the week, they no longer need to rest on Shabbat.

Moshe descended from Mount Sinai to give the Jewish people the second set of tablets on Yom Kippur. Yom Kippur fell on a Monday. The Jewish people may have thought that since they had already rested

---

13. *Tiferet Yehonatan*

on Yom Kippur, there would be no obligation to keep the coming Shabbat; therefore, the second set of tablets had to specifically state that one must always rest on Shabbat even if Yom Kippur had occurred earlier in the week.[14]

Shabbat with Joy

The Talmud (Shabbat 118b) states that whoever keeps the Shabbat properly, even if he was an idol worshipper like the generation of Enoch, his sins will be forgiven. Why does the Talmud single out the generation of Enoch?

Rambam (Maimonides), in Laws of Idolatry 1:1, has a lengthy discussion on how idol worship evolved. He writes that in the days of Enoch, the sons of men erred exceedingly. The advice of the wise men of that generation was nullified, and even Enoch himself was among the victims of that folly. Their mistake was this: Seeing, they said, that God created these stars and planets to rule the world, that He placed them high above to share honors with them, for they are ministers who render service in His presence, it is proper that they be praised and glorified and honored; this is the will of God, to exalt and honor him whom He exalted and honored, even as a king desires to honor those who stand in his presence, for such is the honor of the king. As soon as this matter was rooted in their heart, they commenced to erect temples in honor of the stars, to offer sacrifices to them, to praise and glorify them in words, and bow down to them to reach the will of God by this evil idea.

Rambam then writes, in the long process of time, there arose among the sons of man false prophets, who asserted that God commanded them saying: "Worship one star, or all of the stars, and offer sacrifices to it, and compound for it thus and such, and erect a temple for it, and hew its image so that all of the people, women and children and the rest of the populace included, bow down to it." He, moreover, describes for them a form that he invented and tells them that this

---

14. *Tiferet Yehonatan*

was the image of the star that was pointed out to him in his prophecy. In this manner, they commenced to draw images in temples, beneath trees, upon mountaintops and elevated places, where they congregated to bow down to them and sermonize to the people, saying, "This image has it in its power to do good and evil, and it is proper to worship it, and be in awe of it."

According to Rambam, there were two stages that ultimately led to idol worship. The first in the times of Enoch, the mistaken belief that God utilized the planets and stars to service the world. The second stage the mistaken belief where God gave independent powers to the planets and stars and they could act as they saw fit.

By observing the Shabbat, we are proclaiming that God created the world in six days and rested on the seventh, thereby disproving that God had given independent powers to the stars and the planets. However, the observance of Shabbat does not negate the belief that God vested in the stars and the planets the ability to run the world—just as we see that a king will have deputies who are in charge of certain aspects of the monarchy.

The star that is connected with the seventh day of the week is called *shabtai*; this star symbolizes melancholy and sadness. This star causes people to feel down and sad.

If a person keeps Shabbat with great joy and happiness, he is thereby refuting the belief that God bestowed upon the stars and planets the independent power in the running of the world. Therefore, the Talmud stated that "whoever keeps the Shabbat properly even if he was an idol worshipper like the generation of Enoch his sins will be forgiven."[15]

Shabbat and the Exodus

Why do we make mention of the exodus from Egypt on Shabbat. The Jewish people were meant to be in Egypt for 430 years. In fact, they were only in Egypt for 210 years. There are those who answer that

---

15. *Yaaroth Devash*

the years of exile began from the birth of Yitzchak. This answer is seemingly incomplete since if one calculates the time from the birth of Yitzchak until the exodus, the Jewish people were in exile for 400 years. We are still missing 30 years.

The Jewish people were meant to be enslaved for six days per week, and Shabbat was meant to be their day of rest. However, the Egyptians made them work on Shabbat. They had to guard the crop and similar forms of work. Therefore, the Jewish people worked more than they were meant to. If one calculates one-seventh (days of the week) of 210 (years of servitude), one gets 30 (years). The missing 30 years were calculated by the work the Jewish people did on Shabbat. Shabbat in a sense speeded up the years of slavery. Therefore, we mention the exodus on the Shabbat.[16]

Shabbat and the Mishkan (Tabernacle)

In the section Vayakhel, the Torah first mentions the prohibition of desecrating the Shabbat and then it mentions the obligation of building the Mishkan. The Talmud explains that the reason these laws are mentioned in the manner that they are is to teach us that the building of the Mishkan does not override the observance of Shabbat, and that it is prohibited to build the Mishkan on Shabbat.

A question is posed: The obligation of building the Mishkan is first mentioned in the section of Terumah. However, there the Torah doesn't precede the obligation to build the Mishkan with the prohibition to desecrate the Shabbat as it does in Vayakhel. Why is this so?

Moshe descended Mount Sinai with the first set of tablets on the 17th of Taamuz. The 17th of Taamuz fell on a Friday. (The first day of Sivan fell on a Monday, the first day of Taamuz fell on a Wednesday, and therefore the 17th of Taamuz fell on a Friday.) That being the case, the Jewish people would have begun observing the Shabbat prior to the building the Mishkan. If Moshe would have first written the obligation to keep Shabbat prior to the obligation of constructing the

---

16. *Yaaroth Devash*

Mishkan, I would not necessarily deduce the reason they are written in this specific order was to teach us that one cannot build the Mishkan on Shabbat. I would have assumed the reason for writing Shabbat first and then the building of the Mishkan was simply because Shabbat was going to begin in a few hours' time and there really was no time to commence the building of the Mishkan. Therefore, in Terumah, there is no mention of observing the Shabbat prior to the laws pertaining to the building of the Mishkan.

The second time Moshe descended Mount Sinai with the second set of tablets was on Yom Kippur. Yom Kippur fell on a Monday. Moshe began teaching the Jewish people the Torah on that Tuesday. Moshe taught the Jewish people the section of Vayakhel where the laws of Shabbat are mentioned before the laws of the Mishkan on the Tuesday.

It would make sense that the first laws Moshe taught the Jewish people would be those laws they had to fulfill immediately, the building of the Mishkan. Shabbat was five days away. Moshe had time to teach them the laws of Shabbat. By Moshe initially teaching them the laws of Shabbat and then teaching them the laws of building the Mishkan, Moshe was teaching them that the building of the Mishkan does not override the Shabbat.[17]

Shabbat and the Angels

The Torah states, "And Moshe was on the mountain for forty days." The Torah then goes on to tell us, "Moshe gathered the Jewish people and taught them the laws of Shabbat." Is there a link between Moshe being on the mountain and the observance of Shabbat?

When Moshe went up the mountain to receive the Torah, the angels complained to God and said, "The Torah should remain in heaven." God instructed Moshe to respond to their challenge. Moshe said to the angels that the Torah commands us to keep Shabbat as a day of rest and asked, "Do you then work that you need a day of rest?"

---

17. *Tiferet Yehonatan*

The link between the two sections is that Moshe was in heaven during the time he defended the right of the Torah to be given to the Jewish people, since the Torah speaks about the laws of Shabbat. Therefore, the very first laws Moshe taught the Jewish people when he descended the mountain was the laws of Shabbat.[18]

Shabbat and the Nations of the World

The Talmud (Shabbat 10b) states that God did not inform the nations of the world about Shabbat. This statement needs to be understood in the following manner:

It is without question that the nations of the world know about Shabbat. Many different religions have also sanctified one of the seven days of the week as a holy day. However, no nations have sanctified the seventh day of the week (Saturday) to be their day of holiness. This is the meaning of the Talmudic statement that God didn't inform the nations about Shabbat, meaning no nation replicated the Jewish people in embracing Shabbat as their day of holiness.[19]

Shabbat Protects the Jewish People

The Talmud (Shabbat 118b) states that had the Jewish people properly observed the first Shabbat that was commanded to them, no nation or tongue would have ever ruled them, as it is stated:

And it happened on the seventh day, some people went out from
the nation to collect and they did not find (Shemot 16:27)

And it is written after they went out to collect manna:

And Amalek came and fought with Israel in Refidim
(Shemot 17:8)

---

18. *Midrash Yehonatan*

19. *Yaaroth Devash*

The observance of Shabbat has protected and continues to protect the Jewish people. Therefore, God didn't allow the nations of the world to choose the Shabbat as their day of rest. Rather they chose Sunday or Friday. The reason being, if the nations would have been able to observe Shabbat, the attribute of strict justice would have had grounds to complain to God and ask why is the observance of Shabbat saving the Jewish people when the nations of the world also observe the Shabbat?[20]

Shabbat and Rain

The Talmud (Shabbat 118b) states that whoever observes the Shabbat properly all his sins will be forgiven. The Talmud (Taanit 7b) states that rain will only fall when the Jewish people's sins are forgiven. These two sections of the Talmud indicate that when the Jewish people observe the Shabbat, God will cause the rain to fall.

This explains a series of verses in the Torah. In Vayikra 26:2, the verse says, "You shall observe my Shabbat." The next verse says, "If you follow My laws and faithfully observe My commandments. I will grant your rains in your seasons." The proximity of these verses are consistent with the statements recorded in the two sections of the Talmud that observance of Shabbat causes rain to fall in its appropriate time.[21]

A One-Time Act

Note: At times, the Midrash may compare two ideas that seemingly have no connection with one another. Scholars will attempt to understand the connection between the two. Further note: Slaughtering an animal is prohibited on Shabbat.

---

20. *Yaaroth Devash*

21. *Midrash Yehonatan*

THE MIDRASH STATES THAT ABRAHAM ASKED HIS WIFE, SARAH, to say that she was Abraham's sister and not say that she was his wife. This is consistent with the law that one may slaughter an animal for a sick person on Shabbat. What is the connection between the two?

Why was Abraham afraid to say that Sarah was his wife? At that time all of humanity were obligated to keep the seven Noahite laws. These laws included the prohibition of murder and the prohibition of illicit relationships. Abraham was afraid that if he informed the Egyptians that they were husband and wife, they would kill him and then there would be no prohibition in their having a physical relationship with Sarah. However, murder is also prohibited. Why would Abraham be more concerned that they would transgress the prohibition of murder than the prohibition of illicit relationships?

If a person is unwell on Shabbat and he needs to eat and there is no kosher food, a person has two options: he can either eat non-kosher food or an animal can be slaughtered and the ill person will eat the meat on Shabbat. The law is for the animal to be slaughtered rather than to eat non-kosher. Why is this preferable?

Slaughtering the animal is prohibited; however, it is a one-time act. Eating non-kosher is prohibited; every time you eat it, you are transgressing a sin. We prefer a person to transgress once rather than transgress many times.

Abraham was concerned that perhaps the enemy would transgress the prohibition of murder, a one-time act, rather than transgressing the prohibition of illicit relationships, which would occur on many occasions. Abraham's reasoning is based on the law that we permit the one-time act of slaughtering an animal on Shabbat. We now understand the connection between Abraham asking Sarah to say that they were brother and sister and the law of feeding a sick person on Shabbat.

The 12 Months and the 12 Tribes

Note: The names of the twelve tribes are Reuven, Shimon, Levi, Yehudah, Yissachar, Zevulun, Yoseph, Binyamin, Dan, Naftali, Gad, and Asher. The names of the twelve months are Tishrei, Cheshvan, Kislev, Tevet, Shevat, Adar, Nisan, Iyar, Sivan, Taamuz, Av, and Elul.

REUVEN CORRESPONDS TO THE MONTH OF TISHREI. When Yoseph was thrown into the pit, Reuven dressed himself in a sackcloth and fasted. God proclaimed that Reuven was the first person to do teshuvah (repent). The month of Tishrei is the month of teshuvah. As the Navi Yeshayahu (Prophet Isaiah) said, *"Dirshu Hashem behimotzei"* ("Seek God when He is found. Call Him when he is near.") The Talmud tells us that God is near and can be found during the month of Tishrei.

Shimon corresponds to the month of Cheshvan, the month when Ya'akov blessed his sons prior to his passing. Concerning Shimon he said, *"Orur apom ki az."* ("Cursed be their wrath for it is mighty.") The Talmud tells us that the flood began in the month of Cheshvan. And during the month of Cheshvan, we begin to ask for rain. We very often refer to rain with the expression *"Gevuros geshomim."* ("The might of the rain.") Therefore, Shimon who was a man of great strength is compared to the month of Cheshvan.

Levi corresponds to the month of Kislev for a number of reasons. During the month of Kislev, the Mishkan was completed and the Levites served in the Mishkan. The Maccabees were descendants of Levi, and during this month, the Maccabees were victorious in reconquering the Temple and they relit the menorah.

Yehudah corresponds to the month of Tevet. Yehudah sinned in the month of Tevet. The kings of Israel were descendants of Yehudah. The capital city of Israel was Jerusalem, and it was during this month that Nebuchadnetzer surrounded the city of Jerusalem.

Yissachar corresponds to the month of Shevat. Yissachar is compared to a tree, and during the month of Shevat, we mark the new year of trees.

Zevulun corresponds to Adar. The *mazal* (spiritual energy) of the month of Adar is a fish. When Moshe blessed the tribe of Zevulun, he said, *"Shefa amim yinoku."* ("The tribe of Zevulun will become wealthy by the fish in the sea.") According to a number of commentaries, Zevulun was a twin with his sister Dinah. When we have a leap year, the extra month is added to the month of Adar.

Yoseph corresponds to the month of Nisan. Concerning Yoseph, the verse says, *"Eidus byehoseph shmo btzeiso al mitzroyim."* ("As a testimony for Yehosoph [Yoseph] He ordained when he went forth over the land of Egypt.") And it was in this month the Jewish people left Egypt.

Binyamin corresponds to the month of Iyar. It was in this month that Shlomo Hamelech (King Solomon) began to build the Beit Hamikdash (temple). And the Beit Hamikdash was built on land that belonged to the tribe of Binyamin.

Dan corresponds to the month of Sivan. The Talmud (Pesachim 4a) records that a certain individual always wanted to resolve his disputes via a Beis Din. The Talmud ascertained that the person must be from the tribe of Dan since the verse (Bereishit 49:16) states, *"Dan yadin amo"* ("The tribe of Dan will judge the people.") The judgment would be based on the Torah, which was given to the Jewish people in the month of Sivan.

Naftali corresponds to the month of Taamuz. Ya'akov said that Naftali is a swift gazelle. Moshe sent spies during the month of Taamuz. One of the necessary qualities of a spy is the ability to travel quickly.

Gad corresponds to the month of Av. The word *Gad* can be translated to mean *mazal*. The mazal of the nations of the world became all powerful during this month, and they were able to destroy the Beit Hamikdash.

Asher corresponds to the month of Elul. When Asher was born, Leah said, "Because of my good fortune, women have declared me fortunate." Therefore, the symbol for the month of Elul is a virgin.[22]

---

22. *Yaaroth Devash* 1:2

Rosh Chodesh

*Aaron said to them, "Remove the golden earrings that are on
the ears of your wives, your sons, and your daughters and bring
them (those earrings) to me." (Shemot 32:20)*

The golden calf was constructed from the precious metals and jewelry
donated by the Jewish people. Why did Aaron insist that they also
donate the women's earrings?

The law is that if a Jewish servant wants to remain in servitude
once his enslavement has concluded, he needs to have his ear pierced,
as it says in the Torah:

*His master shall bring him (the slave) to the judges, and he
shall bring him to the door or the doorpost, and his master
shall bore his ear with an awl, and he shall serve him forever.*
(Shemot 21:6)

The servant's master would then place an earring in the servant's
ear, thereby identifying him as his slave. Likewise, women wore earrings to display their subservience to their husbands.

The Talmud (Sanhedrin 63b) records that the reason the Jewish
people wanted to construct the golden calf was because they believed
that by building the golden calf, the laws of illicit relationships would
no longer be applicable. Therefore, Aaron told the Jewish men to bring
their wives' earrings because, if the laws of illicit relationships were
annulled, their wives would no longer be considered subservient to
them and they should no longer wear the earrings they had given them.

The Jewish women did not want to hand over their earrings to their husbands as they were aware of what the earrings symbolized. They did not want the Jewish people to become a nation that did not uphold the sanctity of marriage. The women said, "We are married to one man. We don't want to become the possession of two men."

For the women's noble act of defiance, they were given Rosh Chodesh—the first of the month as their unique festival. Why specifically were the women rewarded with the festival of Rosh Chodesh because of what had occurred with the golden calf?

The Jewish months follow the lunar cycle. Over the course of the month, the moon grows in appearance until the fifteenth day of the month, and then it begins to wane until the end of the month. The Talmud (Chullin 60b) relates that, at the time of creation, the sun and the moon were equal luminaries in the heavens. The moon then complained to God and said, "It is not appropriate for two kings to use the same crown. One of us must be subservient to the other." God therefore said to the moon, "If so go and diminish yourself."

The women said we cannot have two husbands, which is similar to the moon's claim that the sun and the moon are like two monarchs, and two monarchs cannot use the same crown.[23]

_____

23. *Tiferet Yehonatan*

Rosh Hashanah

GOD EXTENDS HIS COMPASSION NOT ONLY TOWARD the Jewish people but also toward the nations of the world. The Talmud (Berachot 7a) states that God is very angry with the kings of the nations who, during the day, remove their crowns and bow down to the sun. Likewise, at night, God becomes very angry when the kings see the moon and bow toward it.

Therefore, God decreed that the Yom Tov of Rosh Hashanah should occur when the moon is not visible and the nations of the world would not be bowing to the moon. This is a great manifestation of God's compassion. God's actions should be a guiding light that we too should show compassion toward all of humanity.[24]

Why We Don't Say Hallel

The Talmud (Rosh Hashanah 32b) states that the reason we don't say Hallel on Rosh Hashanah is because the book of life and the book of death are opened before God. Since the day is such a serious one, a person wouldn't be in the correct frame of mind to say Hallel.

There is another statement recorded in the Talmud (Rosh Hashanah 16b) that on Rosh Hashanah the Jewish people are immediately inscribed in the book of life. If this is the case, why don't we say Hallel on Rosh Hashanah?

Even though the Talmud states that, on Rosh Hashanah, we are inscribed in the book of life, we don't say Hallel on Rosh Hashanah because the final day of judgment occurs on Yom Kippur.[25]

---

24. *Keshet Yehonatan*

25. *Ahavat Yehonatan, Shvii shel Pesach*

Zochreinu L'Chaim

On Rosh Hashanah, we add the following prayer:

> *May we be remembered for life (Zochreinu L'Chaim).*
> *For your sake, the eternal G-d.*

How are we to understand this prayer? What benefit to God is there whether we live or die that we couch our request in terms of "for Your sake"?

There are two reasons a person wants to live: The first being, if a person lives, they can continue enjoying the pleasures of this world. They want to live for selfish reasons. Another reason a person wants to live is to continue doing the will of God.

As King David writes in Tehillim (Psalms) 115:17:

> *Neither will the dead praise God, nor all those who*
> *descend to the grave.*

Likewise, in Pirkei Avot (Ethics of the Fathers) 4:17, it states:

> *It is better to be able to perform God's mitzvoth in this world*
> *even for a short period of time than all of the world to come.*

We can now understand the prayer of *Zochreinu*. We are asking God to please give us life. Because if we live, we will not spend our days indulging ourselves in worldly pleasures; rather, we will spend our time performing Your mitzvoth.[26]

Shofar

The Talmud (Rosh Hashanah 26a) states that any horn can be used as a shofar except for the horn of a cow. The reason is that all horns are formed as one piece, unlike the horn of a cow, which is formed from many pieces. This is to impress upon us the oneness of God.[27]

---

26. *Yaaroth Devash* 1:14

27. *Ahavat Yehonoson Shvii shel Pesach*

Gold on a Shofar

Note: There is a concept in Jewish law that a prosecutor cannot become a defendant. The example given is gold.

The shofar is used on Rosh Hashanah to remind God of the virtues of the Jewish people and that God should forgive them. The following question is posed: Can one place gold on the shofar to beautify it? The answer given is no.

Why? Because gold was used in the making of the golden calf (prosecutor), it cannot be used in defending the Jewish people by placing it on the shofar (defender). It is interesting to note that the Mishkan (Tabernacle) was constructed as an atonement for the sin of the golden calf, and gold was used extensively in the construction of the Mishkan and its vessels.

We can resolve this question by distinguishing between an act of an individual and the act of a community. This principle that "a prosecutor cannot become a defendant" applies only to an individual and not to a community. Therefore, the individual may not place gold on his shofar. However, a community can use gold such as in the construction of the Mishkan as an atonement for the golden calf.[28]

The distinction between the individual and the community applies to another law. The Torah prohibits the lighting of a fire in a person's home. (Shemot 35:3). While in the Mishkan, fire was used on the altar on Shabbat. Why the distinction? Shabbat is an atonement for the sin of the golden calf. Fire was used in the construction of the golden calf. Therefore, an individual on Shabbat cannot light a fire since a "prosecutor cannot become a defender." However, a community (such as the service in the Mishkan) can use fire on Shabbat since the rule of "a prosecutor cannot become a defender" doesn't apply to a community.[29]

---

28. *Tiferet Yehonatan*

29. *Tiferet Yehonatan*

Yom Kippur:
The Ten Days of Repentance

Note: Chol HaMoed are the interim days between the first and last days of the Yom Tov of Pesach and Sukkot.

Navi Yeshayahu (Prophet Isaiah) writes:

Seek out God where He can be found. (Yeshayahu 55:6)

The Talmud (Rosh Hashanah 18a) explains the verse to be referring to the ten days of repentance. Rabbi Isaac Luria (the Arizal) writes that a person should consider these days as being days similar to Chol HaMoed. On Chol HaMoed, only work that prevents a financial loss is permitted. Therefore, I will not write lengthy discourses; rather, I will write about matters that will awaken a person in their service of God.

The seven days between Rosh Hashanah and Yom Kippur correspond to the seven days of the week. This means on the Sunday of the ten days of repentance, a person should do teshuvah for all the Sundays of the year. The same will be true on the Monday etc.[30]

Kaparot

The Shulchan Aruch writes on Erev Yom Kippur, a person should take a rooster and have it slaughtered. The reason being, if the heavenly court has judged a person harshly, the punishment should be placed on

---

30. *Yaaroth Devash* 1:1

the slaughtered animal. This custom is a very ancient one. However, many people spend a lot of money to ensure that the rooster is white. This practice is foolish. The extra money spent purchasing a white rooster would be better spent by giving it to the poor. Idol worshippers would only use white roosters for their service. Therefore, paying more money to purchase a white rooster would be prohibited as it would be imitating the practice of idol worshippers.[31]

Eating on Erev Yom Kippur

Other faiths see separating one's self from worldly pleasures as a means to reach lofty spiritual heights. The Torah, however, never demands things that are harsh and difficult to accomplish. We are commanded to refrain from eating only one day in the calendar year—that day being Yom Kippur. The Torah, which is concerned for our well-being, commands that we eat on Erev Yom Kippur and our eating will be considered a mitzvah. Why is there a mitzvah to eat on Erev Yom Kippur?

All the *aveiros* (sins) of mankind can be traced back to the sin of Adam and Chava when they ate from the tree of knowledge. A person is obligated to rectify their sin. If a person does an *aveiro* (commits a sin), how do we know whether or not he has done *teshuva* (repentance)? The Talmud (Yoma 86b) answers that if a person is in a similar situation as when he sinned and does not sin again, this indicates the person has done teshuva. For example, if a person eats non-kosher and now doesn't eat at all, we cannot be assured that he will not eat non-kosher once he resumes eating. If, however, he does eat and eats only kosher food, we can be assured he has done teshuvah.

Adam and Chava sinned by eating prohibited food. We correct their sin by only eating foods that are permitted. That is why we are obligated to eat on Erev Yom Kippur (and we eat kosher food) to rectify the sin of Adam and Chava.[32]

---

31. *Keshet Yonason*
32. *Yaaroth Devash* 1:1

Inappropriate Thoughts

During the course of the year, a person is not punished for inappropriate thoughts. However, on Yom Kippur, a person *is* punished for inappropriate thoughts. Such thoughts would include jealousy and hatred of a fellow Yid. This is alluded to in the Torah:

> For on this day He shall effect atonement for you to cleanse
> yourself. Before Hahem you shall be cleansed from all your sins.
> (Vayikra 16:30)

The verse says, "Before God you shall be cleansed." Even those sins that only God could know of, such as inappropriate thoughts, one must ensure that one is cleansed from them on Yom Kippur.

The Tenth of the Month

Adam sinned on Friday, the sixth day of creation. God did not speak to him for seven days. The seven days commenced on the Sunday and concluded the following Shabbat. The Sunday after the Shabbat, God once again spoke to Adam. That Sunday was the tenth day of the month. This explains why we mark Yom Kippur on the tenth of the month; it was on the tenth of the month that God once again spoke to Adam.[33]

---

33. *Ahavat Yehonatan*

Sukkot

THE FESTIVAL OF SUKKOT IS CELEBRATED soon after Rosh Hashanah and Yom Kippur. Just as Rosh Hashanah and Yom Kippur are days dedicated to doing *teshuvah* (repentance), Sukkot has an element of teshuvah as well. The Talmud (Sukkah 2a) states that during the festival of Sukkot, one should leave one's home, which is a permanent structure, and move into a sukkah, which is a temporary abode. By doing so, one is in a sense going into exile. This will impress upon the person that our lives here on earth should be viewed as a temporary experience.

Throughout one's life, one should direct their attention toward the heavens, toward God. That is why the *sechach* (the covering of the sukkah) should have gaps in it to allow the person sitting in it to see the stars in heaven.

A truly righteous man will recognize that we are in exile not just for the seven days of Sukkot but for our whole lives; the world is only a temporary abode.

Our forefathers Abraham, Yitzchak, and Ya'akov did not build palaces to live in; rather, they always lived in tents, signifying that they understood that this world is a temporary abode.

Bilaam proclaimed about the Jewish people:

How good are the tents of Ya'akov (Bamidbar 24:5)

Bilaam was not passing judgment on the physical homes the Jewish people lived in during the forty years in the desert; rather, he was proclaiming that the Jewish people were acknowledging that they understood this world is a temporary abode by living in tents.

Chanukah

The Miracle

In the Al HaNissim (prayer said on Chanukah), we list the miracles of Chanukah. One of the miracles is that the large Greek army fell into the hands of the Jewish army, which was small in number. Why is this considered a miracle? Throughout history, there have been many occasions when a small army has been victorious over a much larger army.

Prior to the miracle of Chanukah, many of the Jews had abandoned their faith. Only a small minority remained loyal to God, and they joined the Maccabees. Since so many Jews had abandoned Judaism, Antiochus (the Greek general) attacked the Jewish people. The multitude of Jews who had sinned did not see this as a sign from God that they should do *teshuvah* (repent).

The miracle of Chanukah was that even though many Jews had left Judaism and did not return and those that remained were few in number, God still saved them from Antiochus's large Greek army.[34]

The Blessings

The Talmud (Shabbat 23b) states that on the first night of Chanukah, we recite three blessings. On the second night, we recite only two blessings. The Talmud asks, "Which blessing do we not say?" The Talmud answers, "We don't say the blessing of Shehechiyanu. The Talmud asks, "Perhaps we should leave out the blessing of Sheoso Nisim (and

---

34. *Yaaroth Devash*

say the blessing of Shehechiyanu)." The Talmud answers, "Every day of Chanukah there was a miracle."

A number of questions can be posed on this section of the Talmud. Why did the Talmud ask which blessing we should leave out? Isn't it obvious we should leave out the blessing of Shehechiyanu since Shehechiyanu is said when you do a mitzvah for the first time in a calendar year? And since we lit the menorah on the first night and said a Shehechiyanu then, when we light on the second night (we are not doing the mitzvah for the first time), it is obvious we should leave out the blessing of Shehechiyanu.

The second question we can ask is, once the Talmud answered that the blessing of Shehechiyanu is left out, why does the Talmud suggest that perhaps the blessing of Sheoso Nisim should be left out? Why doesn't the Talmud want to accept the answer that Shehechiyanu is left out and feels it needs to find another answer? Furthermore, didn't the Talmud know that every day of Chanukah had a miracle? How could the Talmud even pose the question of leaving out the blessing Sheoso Nissim in the first place?

It is well known the question posed by the Bet Yoseph, who asks, "Why do we celebrate Chanukah for eight days when the miracle was only for seven days?" When the Cohen found the pure jug of oil, there was enough oil in the jug to burn for one day. The miracle began on the second night when there was no more oil and it still burned for another seven days.

The Turei Zahav answers that, at the end of the first day, even though the jug of oil should have been empty, a small amount of oil remained, which was a miracle; all the oil should have been consumed. Therefore, the miracle was for eight days.

Perhaps we can offer another reason why we celebrate Chanukah for eight days.

The Bet Yoseph asks another question. Every festival is celebrated as one day in Israel, while in the diaspora, it is celebrated as two days (we always add an extra day). Why don't we celebrate Chanukah in the diaspora in the same manner we celebrate all the other festivals to which we add an extra day? Shouldn't we celebrate Chanukah for nine days?

These two questions posed by the Bet Yoseph—first, the miracle was only seven days, and second, we should add an extra day and celebrate Chanukah for nine days—actually answer each other. In truth, the miracle was only for seven days. Why then do we celebrate eight days? Since in the diaspora we always add an extra day to the festivals, we add an extra day to the seven days of Chanukah and we celebrate eight days.

According to this answer, we should recite Shehechiyanu on the second night as well. Similar to what we do by every other festival in the diaspora where we make Shehechiyanu on both nights of the festival?

We will now be able to understand the ebb and flow of the Talmud when it discusses which blessing is not said on the second night.

The Talmud did not know which blessing is omitted on the second night, and it therefore asks which blessing is not recited? It answers the blessing of Shehechiyanu. By answering Shehechiyanu, the Talmud must be of the opinion that the reason we celebrate Chanukah for eight days is not because we added an extra day in the diaspora. Because if that would be the reason for the eight days, then on the second night you must say Shehechiyanu, as we do for every other festival in the diaspora where we make a Shehechiyanu on the first two nights.

If this is the Talmud's position, then the Bet Yoseph's first question remains why celebrate Chanukah for eight days the miracle was for only seven days.

In fact, that is the Talmud's question when it suggests that perhaps we shouldn't say the blessing of Sheoso Nissim on the second night since the miracle was for only seven days and not eight days.

Shabbat Shekalim

Note: The half shekel was a coinage used in Biblical times.

The Yalkut (Ki Tissa 386) quotes the verse:

> *This they shall give, everyone who goes through*
> *the counting.*

Moshe asked God who would be obligated to give the half shekel? God responded that everyone who passed through the water (will be obligated to give).

There are a number of reasons given why the Jewish people were obligated to give a half a shekel. The half a shekel was to atone for the sin of the golden calf. Another reason given, was because the brothers had sold Yoseph into slavery. A third reason given was because, when the Jewish people left Egypt, they spent an unduly amount of time gathering the spoils of the Egyptians from the Reed Sea.

Who had to give the half a shekel will be dependent on the various reasons given for the half a shekel.

If the reason was to atone for the sin of the golden calf, then the tribe of Levi should not be obligated to give a half shekel since the tribe of Levi did not dance around the golden calf. If the reason was because the brothers had sold Yoseph, then the tribes of Reuven and Binyamin should not be obligated to give, since Reuven and Binyamin did not participate in the sale. If, however, the reason is because of the sin of spending too much time in gathering the spoils, then all of the Jewish People would be obligated to give.

We can now fully understand the discussion that took place between Moshe and God quoted above. Moshe was not asking who will give. Moshe knew that everyone had to give. Moshe was asking what is the *reason* for *everyone* being obligated to give? To which God responded that everyone who crossed the sea had to give because they spent too much time collecting the spoils of the Egyptians.[35]

---

35. *Tallelei Oros*

Zayin Adar

Day of Moshe's Passing

Moshe's *neshamah* (soul) did not want to leave Moshe's physical body until it was assured that it would not need to return and be reincarnated in another person's body. The reason why Moshe's neshamah did not want to return was because it did not believe there could be a physical body as pure and holy as the body of Moshe.

Why did Moshe's neshamah think that it would have to return? Moshe had not been allowed to enter the Land of Israel (Eretz Yisrael) with the rest of the Jewish nation. Moshe was unable to fulfill the many mitzvoth that could be fulfilled only in Eretz Yisrael. Moshe's neshamah thought it would have to return and fulfill those mitzvot that it had not been able to accomplish while it was in Moshe's body.

Moshe reassured his neshamah that it would not have to return since God would consider it as if he had fulfilled all 613 mitzvot even those mitzvot could only be fulfilled in in the Eretz Yisrael.

Based on this, we can understand a somewhat difficult statement recorded in the Talmud (Sotah 13b). The Talmud states that Moshe did not pass away. How are we to understand this statement when the Torah speaks in great detail about the passing of Moshe? We can interpret the statement "Moshe did not pass away" to mean that Moshe's neshamah would not have to return in another person's body.[36]

---

36. *Yaaroth Devash* 2:6

Birth of New Jewish Leader

The Talmud (Megillah 13b) tells us that Haman casted lots to see which month would be the opportune month to destroy the Jewish people. When Haman saw that the month of Adar had been chosen, he was delighted since it was in the month of Adar that Moshe had passed away. And just as Moshe passed away in Adar so to would the Jewish people all perish in the month of Adar.

The Talmud points out the error in Haman's thinking. While it is true that Moshe passed away in Adar, Moshe was also born in the month of Adar. The month of Adar is really a joyous month and no harm will befall the Jewish people in such a happy month.

We can ask two questions on the above quoted Talmud: Why is it that Haman knew when Moshe passed away, yet he did not know when he was born? And, even if Haman knew when Moshe was born, it should be of little consequence in comparison to the date when he passed away. As we see that there are many who have the custom to fast on a *yahrtzeit* (the date when a person passed away) even if the yahrtzeit falls on the same day the person was born. Clearly then the date of death is of greater consequence than the date of a person's birth.

Shlomo Hamelech (King Solomon) in Kohelet writes:

The sun sets and the sun rises.

God never leaves the world without righteous leaders. It is also of worth noting that the Talmud will sometimes call a rabbi with the name Moshe and not by the name given to them at birth. Rashi clarifies this anomaly by explaining that any *Talmid Chacham* (Torah Scholar) can be called Moshe. Likewise the Arizal writes that a Talmid chacham has a spark of Moshe's neshamah.

We can now appreciate Haman's mistake. Haman may have actually known when Moshe was born and that he passed away on the same day. Haman was also aware that the day of Moshe's passing is of more significance than the day of Moshe's birth. And since Moshe passed away on 7th of Adar, the fact that Moshe was born on the 7th of Adar is insignificant.

However, what Haman did not know was that on the very same day Moshe passed away, another great Jewish leader was born, and in the merit of this new Jewish leader, the Jewish people would be protected.

We can now offer an ingenious interpretation of the Talmudic statement that Haman didn't realize when Moshe was born. The Talmud was not referring to the birthday of Moshe. Rather, it was referring to the great Jewish leader who was born on the very day that Moshe passed away. And every great Jewish leader can be called Moshe. And in the merit of this new Jewish leader, the Jewish people will be saved.[37]

---

37. *Yaaroth Devash* 1:3

Shabbat Zachor

Note: On Shabbat Zachor we read the section of the Torah that commands us to remember the evil of Amalek and to eradicate it from the face of the earth.

KING SAUL WAS COMMANDED TO DESTROY THE AMALEKITES. King Saul instructed each of his soldiers to take a lamb, and by counting the lambs, he would then know how many soldiers he had for the battle against Amalek.

The Targum explains that the lambs were used for the Korbon Pesach since the war took place during Pesach. God wanted to destroy the Amalekites during the month of Nisan to show the world His greatness. Amalek was the greatest sorcerer among the nations, and the sheep was his mazel, and he was still unable to defeat the Jewish people.[38]

---

38. *Ahavas Yehonatan* Zachor

Purim

A Double Miracle

What is considered a miracle? A miracle is an occurrence that does not follow the laws of nature. However, if what occurs follows the laws of nature, the event is not considered a miracle.

By way of example: When the Jewish people traveled through the Reed Sea, they experienced the miracle of the splitting of the sea. It was a miracle because they were able to pass on dry land that, moments before, had been a raging sea. However, that the Egyptians were drowning at the same time is not considered a miracle. Since the law of nature is that when people are thrown into a raging sea, they will drown.

Similarly, in Sefer Melachim (Book of Kings), we are told that Sancheriv had 185,000 soldiers and was planning to attack the Jewish people. And in one night all of his soldiers died. Such an occurrence is definitely miraculous.

As a result of this miracle, King Chizkiyahu and the Jewish people were able to live in peace and tranquility. The Jewish people living in peace is not considered miraculous. The nature is that when a nation is no longer surrounded by its enemy, it will be able to live in peace.

The story of Purim could have unfolded three different ways: Achashverosh could have nullified his decree, thus saving the Jewish People; however, Haman would have remained all powerful. Achashverosh could have killed Haman, and the Jewish people would have retained the same lowly status that they held prior to the evil decree. What unfolded was a double miracle. First, Haman was killed, and second, the position of the Jewish people was elevated. Mordechai was given a very lofty position, and many of the gentiles sought to become Jewish because the fear of the Jewish people was upon them.[39]

Queen Esther

The Talmud (Megillah 13a) writes that Esther's Jewish name given to her at birth was Hadassah. It was only later in life due to her behavior that she was called Esther. Why then is the Megillah called Megilat Esther and not Megilat Hadassah?

The Talmud (Hullin 139b) states that the name Esther is derived from the following verse:

And I will hide my face (Devarim 31:18)

This is implying that God had concealed himself as the miracle of Purim was unfolding. This is why the Megillah is called Megilat Esther, to impress upon the Jewish people that even though God was concealed, He still performed the Purim miracle.

Rejoicing on Purim

It is true that Haman was put to death and the decree to kill all the Jewish people was annulled. However, Haman's successors have been persecuting and killing Jewish people simply because they are Jewish people throughout the generations.

If so, why do we rejoice on Purim? We rejoice because God has commanded us to do so. We are b'simcha (truly happy) because on the day of Purim, we accepted the Torah anew. And on the day of Purim, we are reminded that God is all merciful toward the Jewish people.[40]

---

39. *Yaaroth Devash* 1:3

40. *Yaaroth Devash* 1:3

Shalosh Regalim
(The Three Festivals)

THE TALMUD (BERACHOT 5B) SAYS THAT GOD gave the Jewish people three gifts: the Torah, Eretz Yisrael (the Land of Israel), and Olam HaBa (the world to come). The three festivals correspond to these three gifts.

Pesach corresponds to Eretz Yisrael since the main purpose of leaving Egypt was to enter Eretz Yisrael. And after the Jewish people wandered in the desert for forty years, on the tenth of Nisan, they entered Eretz Yisrael.

Shavuot corresponds to the Torah. The Jewish people received the Torah on Shavuot.

Sukkot corresponds to Olam HaBa. Navi Yeshaya (Prophet Isaiah) says that during the period of Olam HaBa when God will punish the wicked with the fiery sun, the shade of the sukkah will protect the righteous.

The Navi Yechezkel (Prophet Ezekiel) tells the Jewish people that when Moshiach will come, they need to remember the Yom Tov of Pesach and the Yom Tov of Sukkot. And all the *korbanot* (sacrifices) offered on Pesach and Sukkot need to be brought during the Messianic era as well.

Why doesn't the Navi instruct the Jewish people concerning the Yom Tov of Shavuot?

The Talmud (Berachot 12b) brings an opinion that when Moshiach will come, we will no longer remember the miracle of the exodus from Egypt. As Navi Yermiyahu (Prophet Jeremiah) writes:

There will come a time when it will no longer be said,
"As God lives, Who brought up the Jewish people from
Egypt." Rather, "As God lives who brought up the Jewish
people from the northland and from all the lands where
He had driven them."

Since the Yom Tov of Sukkot is to remind us of the clouds of glory that protected us when we left Egypt, we may have thought we no longer need to mark the Yomim Tovim of Pesach and Sukkot; therefore, the Navi mentions them specifically, unlike the Yom Tov of Shavuot, which isn't directly connected with the exodus from Egypt.

Nisan

In Yechezkel 45:18, the prophet writes:

God said in the first month on the first of the month you shall take a young bull without blemish and you shall purify the altar.

There is an argument recorded in the Talmud (Rosh Hashanah 8a) over when was the world created. One opinion says the world was created in Tishrei, while the other opinion says the world was created in Nisan.

Perhaps one can say that there is no argument between these two opinions and they are referring to different worlds. The Midrash (Bereishit Rabbah 3:7) states that God created many worlds and destroyed them. These worlds became *tohu va vohu* (an expression of emptiness and desolation) and then God created the world as we know it. Both opinions will agree that the worlds that were destroyed were created in Tishrei while the world as we know it that will be everlasting was created in Nisan.

When we mark Rosh Hashanah in the month of Tishrei, we are celebrating the creation of the world of *tohu* (a world that is not everlasting). However, when Moshiach does come, the world will be everlasting and we will mark Rosh Hashanah on the first of Nisan.

The Navi Yechezkel, when he spoke about bringing a *korbon* (sacrifice) on the first day of the first month, he was referring to the month of Nisan after the coming of Moshiach.

Pesach

The Choice

The Midrash (Bereishit Rabah 44:21) states that God offered Abraham two options concerning the future of the Jewish people. Either they will be exiled and in servitude to another nation or go to Gehenom (hell). Abraham was unsure which to choose. God advised him to choose exile.

Abraham's dilemma was, if the Jewish people will be sent into exile, perhaps they will sin and abandon God and will have to go to Gehenom. If this is the case, the Jewish people would suffer two forms of punishment: exile *and* Gehenom.

God suggested that Abraham choose exile since He knew the Jewish people would never fully abandon Him. And, in fact, they would leave the exile of Egypt *birchush gadol* (with great wealth). The great wealth refers to all the sparks of holiness trapped in Egypt.

Servitude in Egypt

When the Jewish people were in Egypt, they caused many Egyptians to believe in God. Pharaoh was worried that perhaps all the Egyptians would believe in God and become part of the Jewish people. When Pharaoh said, "Perhaps the Jewish people will multiply (*pen yarbo*)," he was referring to the Egyptians who would become part of the Jewish people. Therefore, Pharaoh forced the Jewish people into slavery. The Egyptians would not want to embrace the Jewish Nation and then be forced into slavery.

God in Exile

God told Abraham: Your children will be in exile for 400 years. However, the Jewish Nation did not remain in Egypt for 400 years. The commentaries explain that the missing years were made up by God being together with the Jewish people in exile. The verse says (referring to Moshe):

Moshe left the city to pray to God.

Rashi explains that Moshe didn't want to pray to God in the city because the city was full of idols. If so, how could God say that He was among the Jewish people during their exile if the place was full of idols?

A Cohen cannot come in contact with a corpse. However, if one of his seven closest relatives passes away, he can become impure. The Torah refers to the Jewish people as "God's children" (*bonim atem*). Therefore, God was able to become impure for the sake of His children.

The unique relationship between God and the Jewish people is alluded to by linking the last verse of Torah reading of Bo and the first verse of Torah reading of Beshalach. The last verse of Bo reads:

God took the Jewish people out of Egypt with a mighty hand.

How was it possible for God to enter a place contaminated with impurity? The first verse of Beshalach answers the question. The verse reads:

When Pharaoh sent the Jewish people out of Egypt God did not lead them via the land of the Pelishtim because it was too close.

The Hebrew word for *close* is *ki karov hu. Ki karov hu* can also be translated to mean a close relative. The two verses now read as follows: God took the Jewish people out of Egypt with a mighty hand. How could God enter Egypt to take the Jewish people out? Since the Jewish people are God's close relative, they are God's children. He was allowed to enter a place filled with idols.

The Missing Thirty Years

The Jewish people were meant to be enslaved in Egypt for 430 years. Even if we calculate the years of exile starting from the birth of Yitzchak, we are still missing thirty years. The Jewish people were enslaved in Egypt for three generations, as the verse says:

> *The fourth generation will return from exile.*

A generation is seventy years. Three times seventy is 210 years. The Jewish people should have been given one day per week as a day of rest. However, they were forced to work on Shabbat and didn't have a day of rest. One-seventh of 210 is 30. These thirty years were added to the 400 years. The Jewish people were enslaved for a total of 430 years.

Brit Milah

The Midrash informs us when the Jewish people were in Egypt they did not circumcise their sons. This is alluded to in the verse (Shemot 6:5) in which God tells Moshe:

> *I also heard the moans of the Jewish people, whom the Egyptians are holding in bondage and I remembered my covenant.*

The words "I remembered my covenant" can be understood to mean "I remembered that the Jewish people did not give their sons a bris and therefore their time in slavery was more difficult than it should have been."

Brotherhood

Moshe sent messengers from Kadesh to the King of Edom:

> *So says your brother, Israel, you know of all the hardship that has befallen us.* (Bamidbar 20:14)

Why does Moshe instruct the messengers to mention that the Jewish people and the Edomites are brothers? Moshe wanted to subtly inform the King of Edom of the tragedy that can unfold when brothers act badly with each other. He was referring to when the brothers sold Yoseph as a slave to the Egyptians.

Like Father Like Son

Moshe was perplexed why the Jewish people were enslaved and made to suffer more so than any other nation. The sons of Ya'akov had sold Yoseph into slavery. They did this because they felt Yoseph had told their father false rumors about them. Therefore, they in turn were punished and had to descend to the land of Egypt.

The Talmud (Berachot 7a) states that children are not punished for the sins of their fathers. If that is the case, why did the descendants of the brothers need to remain in servitude in Egypt? The Talmud explains that if the children follow in the footsteps of their fathers, they too will be punished accordingly.

Moshe had killed an Egyptian who had struck a Jewish slave. He then was confronted by a Jew who was quarreling with another Jew and was about to strike him. And Moshe said to him, "Why are you going to strike your friend?" The Jew replied, "Do you plan to slay me as you have slain the Egyptian?" Moshe became very frightened that this Jew would go and inform on him to the Egyptian authorities. Moshe responded:

Indeed the matter has become known to me. (Shemot 2:14)

Moshe's response "Indeed the matter has become known to me" can be understood to mean that Moshe now realized why the Jewish people had remained in exile. Tragically, the Jewish people were informers, just as the children of Ya'akov had been. They were following in their footsteps and therefore they remained in exile.

Our Forefathers Were in Exile

The years of exile were counted from the birth of Yitzchak. A question can be asked: What form of exile did our forefathers experience? Even though they were living in Israel, they were constantly afraid of being attacked by their enemies. Yitzchak was afraid of being attacked by Yishmael, and Ya'akov by his brother Esau. As we see by Ya'akov, the verse says:[41]

> *Then they traveled and the fear of God was upon the cities that were around them, so they did not pursue Ya'akov's sons.*
> (Bereishit 35:5)

God Sent Moshe

At the time of the exodus from Egypt, God asked Moshe to go down to Egypt and redeem the Jewish people. Initially, Moshe refused and felt that God Himself should redeem the Jewish people.

God knew if He would reveal Himself to the Jewish people, they would perish from the fear of suddenly seeing God's presence. Therefore, God first sent Moshe to inform the Jewish people that God was coming to redeem them. He then performed many miracles to prepare the Jewish people for God's revelation (on Mount Sinai).[42]

Pharaoh's Miscalculation

Pharaoh didn't believe the Jewish people were ready for the final redemption. If Pharaoh would have known that the Jewish people would have to endure other exiles besides the exile from Egypt, he would not have made such a mistake.

Moshe asked God, "If the Jewish people will ask who sent me, what should I tell them?" God answered:

---

41. *Tiferet Yehonatan*

42. *Tiferet Yehonatan*

*You should tell the Jewish people, "I will be with them in
this exile and I will be with them in their other exiles."*
(Shemot 3:14)

Moshe answered God that it would be too much for them to bear
if he tells them that they will have to endure further exiles. God agreed
with Moshe and instructed him to only inform the Jewish people that
God would be with them during this exile.

We can now appreciate what God meant when He told Moshe,
*"When you speak to Pharaoh tell him **everything** that I said."* Meaning,
unlike when you speak to the Jewish people and you will inform them
only of their present exile, when you speak to Pharaoh you should
inform him that the Jewish people will endure other exiles. And he
should not make the mistake in believing the Jewish people still need to
endure the exile in Egypt.[43]

Moshe's Difficulty Speaking

*Moshe said before God, "Behold, I am of closed lips;
so how will Pharaoh listen to me?"* (Shemot 6:30)

Moshe's prophecy was such that God spoke through Moshe. Moshe
was like a speaker through which God's words were heard. If so, what
was Moshe's concern? Undoubtedly, God's message would be heard
loud and clear even if Moshe had difficulty speaking!

God's prophecy was spoken in *Lashon Hakodesh* (Hebrew), the
language familiar to the Jewish people. However, Pharaoh only understood Egyptian. Moshe would have to translate God's words into
Egyptian. Moshe was concerned that he would be unable to adequately
express God's words in Egyptian.

Another explanation is that Moshe was concerned that Pharaoh
would perhaps think that if God is all mighty, how is it that He sends
a messenger who is unable to articulate his words properly? Wouldn't

---

43. *Tiferet Yehonatan*

an all-mighty God cure him before He sent him? And since God didn't heal him, we must say that he isn't a messenger of God.

"The Jewish People Have Not Listened to Me"

Moshe spoke before God saying, "Behold, the Children of Israel have not listened to me, so how will Pharaoh listen to me? And I have closed lips," (Shemot 6:12)

In his commentary on this verse, Rashi writes that this is one of ten *kal vachomers* that appear in the Torah.

Note: A kal vachomer *is a logical argument that reasons: If a rule or fact applies in a situation where there is relatively little reason for it to apply, certainly it applies in a situation where there is more reason for it to apply.*

In the verse quoted, Moshe reasons that if the Jewish people for whom his message will benefit don't listen to him, why would Pharaoh to whom the message is detrimental listen to him?

We could suggest that the *kal vachomer* is not applicable in this case, since the Torah says that the reason the Jewish people didn't listen to Moshe was because of *mikotzer ruach* (shortness of wind and hard work). (Shemot 6:9) Pharaoh was not enslaved and therefore perhaps he would listen to the words of Moshe.

The Torah says the Jewish people would not listen to Moshe because of the hard work. The Midrash explains the "hard work" to mean idol worship. The Jewish people would not listen to Moshe because they were worshipping idols. If this is the understanding of "hard work," Moshe's concern is a valid one. His concern was that if the Jewish people would not listen to him because they were serving idols, how much more so would Pharaoh not listen to him since Pharaoh considered himself to be an actual idol?

Why was Moshe concerned that the Jewish people would not listen to him? If a person hears good news, why wouldn't the person believe it? The Jewish people were under the impression that the redemption from Egypt would be the ultimate redemption. The Jewish people would leave Egypt, receive the Torah, and enter Eretz Yisrael with Moshiach.

The Jewish people were well aware of the *brachot* (blessings) that Ya'akov had given his sons. The *bracha* given to Yehudah was *lo yosur shevet miyehuda* (the scepter shall not depart from Yehudah, nor the student of the law from between his feet), until Shiloh comes and to him will be a gathering of people.

The ultimate redeemer Moshiach will be a descendant from the tribe of Yehudah. Moshe was from the tribe of Levi, and he felt the Jewish people wouldn't listen to him since he wasn't from the tribe of Yehudah.[44]

The Redeemer Will Come from Shevet Levi

Shevet Levi (the tribe of Levi) was not subjugated in Egypt. By using witchcraft, Pharaoh was able to see that the redeemer of the Jewish people would be from the tribe of Levi. Pharaoh felt that the redeemer could not be someone who had not been enslaved in Egypt. He therefore did not enslave the Levites. In fact, it was for this reason that the Jewish people did not believe Moshe when he declared that he had come to redeem the Jewish people.

Why was the redeemer designated to come from the tribe of Levi? The Egyptians claimed that the Jewish people were unable to prove that their lineage is 100 percent pure. If the Egyptians were able to enslave the Jewish people, how much more so they were able to enslave the Jewish women. Therefore, the redeemer would need to be someone who was of pure descent. The redeemer would therefore have to come from the tribe of Levi as the Levites, both men and women were not enslaved.[45]

---

44. *Tiferet Yehonatan*

45. *Tiferet Yehonatan*

God Is Truly Compassionate

So said the Lord the G-d of the Jewish people, How long will
you refuse to humble yourself Before Me? (Shemot 10:3)

Why indeed did Pharaoh not listen to God? Pharaoh felt that God
was the source of all goodness and was full of compassion and no evil
could emanate from Him. Therefore, he didn't believe that God would
punish him and, as a result, he didn't listen to God's warning.[46]

Korban Pesach to Be Brought in Afternoon

The Torah tells us that the *korban Pesach* (paschal lamb) was to be
brought in the afternoon:

The entire congregation of the community of Israel shall
slaughter it (korban Pesach) in the afternoon. (Shemot 12:6)

Why was it to be brought specifically in the afternoon?

If the Jewish people brought the sacrifice at night, the Egyptians
would claim that the Jewish people were unable to bring it during
the day since the Egyptians worshipped the sun as a god. Likewise, if
the Jewish people brought the sacrifice by day, the Egyptians would
claim that the Jewish people couldn't bring it at night since Egyptians
worshipped the moon. Therefore, the Jewish people were instructed
to bring it in the afternoon when both the sun and the moon were
present.[47]

Korban Pesach to Be Eaten Before Midnight

Why weren't the Jewish people allowed to eat the korban Pesach after
midnight? At midnight, the firstborn of the Egyptians began to die and
even a firstborn Egyptian that was in the house of a Jew also died. The

---

46. *Tiferet Yehonatan*

47. *Ahavas Yehonatan*

Talmud (Yevamot 61a) states that a gentile conveys impurity. For the korban Pesach to be eaten in a state of purity, it had to be consumed before the firstborn Egyptians would die, which was at midnight.[48]

Plague of the Firstborn

I will smite every firstborn in the land of Egypt, both man and beast, and upon all the gods of Egypt will I wreak judgments I, the Lord. (Shemot 12:12)

God did not send a *malach* (an angel) to kill the firstborn of the Egyptians as we read in the Haggadah, *ani vlo malach* (I [smote] and not an angel).

Why didn't God send an angel to kill the firstborn of the Egyptians?

In truth, all the Egyptians deserved to be killed; the whole nation had persecuted the Jewish people, not just the firstborn. God in His infinite compassion spared the whole nation and poured His wrath only on the firstborn. If God would have sent an angel, the angel would have killed the whole nation, as the angel would not have been able to distinguish between the firstborn and the rest of the nation.[49]

It Was Midnight

It was at midnight and God. . . (Shemot 12:29)

The Zohar (2:38) explains that even though it was midnight, the sun was shining as if it were midday. Why does the Zohar say that the sun was shining at midnight?

The Midrash in Bereishit Rabbah 3:6 says that God does not attach His name to a curse. This can be deduced from the following verse:

---

48. *Chasdai Yehonatan*

49. *Tiferet Yehonatan*

God called the light day and the darkness He called night.
(Bereishit 1:5)

When discussing the light, the verse says, "God called the light day." However, when the verse discusses darkness, the verse says that He called it night. It didn't say, "and God called the darkness night."

The reason the verse didn't mention God's name by darkness is because darkness is a curse, and God doesn't attach His name to a curse. If God doesn't attach His name to darkness, why in the verse does it say, "It was at midnight and God . . ."?

The Zohar resolves this question by explaining, in truth. it wasn't dark at all; the sun was shining as if it was in the middle of the day.[50]

Exodus from Egypt

And it was when Pharaoh sent the nation (out of Egypt)
(Shemot 13:17)

The Torah uses the word *vayehi*, meaning "when it was." The Midrash tells us that both Moshe and the Jewish people claimed, "Woe is upon us!" Why were Moshe and the Jewish people so distraught that they used words of sorrow?

The Zohar tells us that whenever the Torah uses the word *"am, nation,"* it means to include the mixed multitude. So when the Jewish people left Egypt, they didn't leave alone—a vast number of non-Jewish people left with them. Since so many non-Jewish people left, this would diminish God's glory as it would appear less miraculous. The reason being no one was ever able to leave Egypt without Pharaoh's permission, and the other nations who left would attribute their leaving to their gods. That is why Moshe and the Jewish people were so distressed.[51]

---

50. *Midrash Yehonatan*

51. *Tiferet Yehonatan*

HAGGADAH

Amar Rebbi Elazar ben Azariah

Rabbi Elazar ben Azariah teaches that the words *kol yemei chayecha* (all the days of your life), show us that we need to say Shema at night. The Chachamim interpret the word *kol* to include the times of Moshiach. Why didn't Rabbi Elazar ben Azariah interpret the words as the Chachamim did to include the times of Moshiach?

Rabbi Elazar ben Azariah is of the opinion that even in the times of Moshiach, we will still keep all the mitzvot. Therefore, it would be unnecessary for the word *kol* to include the Messianic era. Since, according to Rabbi Elazar ben Azariah, there is no distinction in terms of the mitzvoth between pre–Messianic era and post–Messianic era. Therefore, he interprets the word *kol* to include our obligation to say the Shema at night.

Baruch Hamakom (Blessed Is God)

There are two opinions why the Jewish people did not remain in Egypt for the full 430 years that had been decreed upon them. One answer given is that they were also enslaved at night. Slaves normally would work only during the day; by working at night, their enslavement period should be cut in half. Another explanation given is that the angels were also in servitude and not only the Jewish people. Therefore, the Jewish people were released earlier as the work that had been decreed was fulfilled quicker due to the input of the angels; more work was done than originally decreed.

The Talmud (Shabbat 88b) states that when Moshe went up to heaven to receive the Torah, the angels argued and requested from God that the Torah remain in heaven. God commanded Moshe to answer the angels. Moshe responded, "What does it say in the Torah? The Torah says that God took the Jewish people out of Egypt." He then said to the angels, "Were you enslaved in Egypt and then freed?"

This section of the Talmud is clearly of the opinion that the angels were not enslaved in Egypt. According to this section of the Talmud, the reason the Jewish people left early is because they worked at night. This will explain why we mention the exodus from Egypt at night because the slavery was at night as well.

We now can understand on a deeper level the connection of these two sections in the Haggadah. The Haggadah states that we are obligated to mention the exodus from Egypt at night and, in the next section, we bless God for giving the Torah to the Jewish people.

If we mention the exodus from Egypt at night, it is because we follow the opinion that they were enslaved at night and not because the angels were enslaved as well. Since the angels weren't enslaved, they have no claim to receive the Torah. And we rightfully proclaim in the next section of the Haggadah, "Blessed is God Who gave the Torah to the Jewish people."

Sacrifice of the Paschal Lamb, Matzah, and Maror

Navi Yermiyahu (Prophet Jeremiah) writes:

> I remember to you the loving kindness of your youth, the love of your nuptials, your following Me in the desert, in a land not sown. (Yermiyahu 2:2)

The night the Jewish people left Egypt, they ate the korban Pesach (paschal lamb) with maror and matzah. These three foods show the tremendous faith the Jewish people had in God that He would sustain them while traveling in the desert.

The korban Pesach had to be roasted. Meat that is roasted is digested quickly; the result is that one becomes hungry more quickly than if he had eaten cooked meat. Likewise, maror helps speed the digestive process, causing one to become hungry sooner. Matzah is made from water and flour, which is not allowed to rise prior to baking the dough. The Jewish people had complete trust in God and were not worried where their next meal would come from. Therefore, they did not hesitate to eat foods that would digest quickly.[52]

---

52. *Ahavat Yehonatan*

The Chacham

When the Torah discusses the question posed by the chacham (wise son), it states:

> If your son asks you in time to come, saying, "What are the testimonies, the statutes, and the ordinances, which the Lord our God has commanded you?" (Devarim 6:20)

Many ask what the difference is between the question posed by the chacham and the one posed by the rasha (wicked son).

The rasha's question implies that he is excluding himself from the rest of the Jewish nation because his question contains the Hebrew word *lochem* (to you) and does not say *lanu* (to us)—meaning "I don't particularly care what you will respond because it doesn't affect me; it only affects *you*." The chacham also phrases his question using the word *eschem* (to you)—implying, as with the question posed by the rasha, that he doesn't care what answer will be given since it doesn't affect him.

There is a slight variance in the question posed by the chacham compared to the question posed by the rasha. The chacham's question contains the word *leimor* (saying). Whenever the Torah uses the word *leimor*—for example, in the often-quoted verse *Vaydaber Hashem . . . leimor* (God spoke to Moshe saying), the verse should be understood to mean that God instructed Moshe that "What I am about to tell you, you should convey to others."

The chacham has no questions. However, he knows many of his friends and acquaintances will more than likely challenge him with matters relating to the exodus from Egypt. The verse is now understood to mean: "When your son will ask you questions posed to him by others and the answers you will give, he will share with them." By using the pronoun *them*, he is not excluding himself. As the word *them* is referring to those who asked the question initially—unlike the rasha, who was asking for himself. When he uses the pronoun *them*, he indeed is excluding himself from the rest of the Jewish nation.[53]

---

53. *Tiferet Yehonatan*

Splitting of the Reed Sea

The Midrash (Bereishit Rabbah 5:5) states that when God created the world, He instructed the Reed Sea to split when the Jewish people passed through it. Why was it necessary for God to make such a condition by the creation?

The Talmud (Shabbat 32a) states that if God performs a miracle for someone, the person will lose some of the reward he was entitled to. If the splitting of the sea was a miracle, the Jewish people would have been upset because they would have lost some their reward. Because God designated the exact moment in time when the sea would split during creation, the splitting of the sea would not be considered a miracle. The Jewish people would not be concerned that the splitting of the sea would take away from the reward due to them.[54]

The Sea Split

King David writes in Tehillim (Psalms) 114:3:

The [Reed] sea saw and fled . . .

The Midrash answers that it saw the *Baraita* (teachings) of Reb Yishmael. How are we to understand the answer given by the Midrash?

When God instructed the waters to split, the sea asked God, "Why should we split? The Jewish people are idol worshippers, and the Egyptians are idol worshippers. Why are the Jewish people being saved and the Egyptians are drowning?"

God responded that the Jewish people did *teshuvah* (repented); therefore, they should be saved. Prior to the giving of the Torah, the Jewish people had the status of a Ben Noach (subject to the Noahite Law). There is an argument whether or not a Ben Noach is able to have his sins nullified by doing teshuvah.

It would seem the Talmud (Yoma 37a) is proof that a Ben Noach's

---

54. *Tiferet Yehonatan*

act of teshuvah will remove his sins. The Talmud quotes a verse in Mishlei (Proverbs) 10:7:

The name of the wicked shall rot.

The verse teaches us we should not name a person with the name of a wicked individual.

The following question can be posed: How was Rabbi Yishmael called Yishmael? Wasn't Yishmael the son of Abraham, a rasha (a wicked person)?

The rabbis answer that Yishmael, son of Abraham (who had the status of a Noahite), did teshuvah, and God accepted his repentance. Therefore, Rabbi Yishmael was named after Yishmael, son of Abraham. This is proof God accepts the act of teshuvah from a Ben Noach.

We can now understand the somewhat ambiguous statement, "What did the sea see that led it to split?" It saw the writings of Rabbi Yishmael.[55]

The Shirah

Note: Shirah is the song sang by Moshe and the Jewish people as they crossed the Reed Sea.

> On that day the Lord saved Israel from the hands of the Egyptians, and Israel saw the Egyptians dying on the seashore. And Israel saw the great hand, which the Lord had used upon the Egyptians, and the people feared the Lord and in Moshe, His servant. (Shemot 14:30–31)

> Then Moshe and the Jewish people sang this song to the Lord, and they spoke, saying. (Shemot 15:1)

The Mekhilta (rabbinic commentary) brings various opinions on why the sea split. One opinion states that it was in the merit of Abraham

---

55. *Midrash Yehonatan*

that caused the water to split. Another opinion is that it was in the merit of the faith the Jewish people had in God that caused the waters to split.

One difference between the two opinions is thus: If they were saved in the merit of Abraham, the Jewish people would not have been permitted to see the Egyptians drown. This can be seen in the Torah's account when Lot and his family were saved from Sodom. The angel tells Lot and his family they were being saved in the merit of Abraham, and they were not allowed to see the downfall of the people of Sodom. Likewise, if the Jewish people were being saved in the merit of Abraham, they too would not be worthy of seeing the Egyptians drown. However, if the Jewish people were being saved because of their faith in God, they would be deserving of seeing the Egyptians drown.

Another difference between the two opinions is: If they were saved in the merit of Abraham, the Jewish people would not be able to sing a song of praise to God. This can be deduced from the Talmud (Sanhedrin 94a, Berachot 10b). The Talmud states that the rabbis were of the opinion that King Chizkiyahu was unable to sing a song of praise to God since he was saved in the merit of King David and not in his own merit. Similarly, if the Jewish people were saved in the merit of Abraham, they could not have sung a song to God.

The verse quoted above can now be understood to mean that God saved the Jewish people from the hands of the Egyptians. They were saved because of their faith in God and not in the merit of Abraham. They therefore were permitted to see the Egyptians drown, and they were able to sing a song of praise to God.

Then Moshe and the children of Israel sang this song to the Lord, and they spoke, saying, I will sing to God, for very exalted is He. (Shemot 15:1)

The Talmud (Sotah 30b) asks how we are to understand "and they spoke, saying"? Who is the verse referring to?

The Jewish people by the Reed Sea reached the level of prophecy to the extent that when Moshe sang the Shirah (song praising God), the

Jewish people simultaneously sang along with Moshe word for word. However, the mixed multitude of non-Jewish people who left Egypt with the Jewish people did not reach a level of prophecy.

We can now understand the statement "and they spoke, saying" to mean that "and they" refers to the Jewish people; they sang the song (in unison with Moshe). *Saying* refers to the mixed multitude; when they heard the song from the Jewish people, they repeated the words and sang the song.[56]

> *The Lord is a Master of war; the Lord is His name.*
> (Shemot 15:3)

Why is God's name mentioned twice?

God has many different names. Each name represents a different quality of God. In this verse, the name Lord represents God of mercy. God's name is mentioned twice to impress upon us that even though God is described as being the Master of war, He went to battle as the God of mercy and compassion.[57]

Another explanation offered is that an angel doesn't have a specific name. The angel's name depends on the mission and task he needs to fulfill. This is not the case by God. His name remains the same irrespective of what He wants to accomplish. As in our case, even though God (God of mercy) is going to war, His name doesn't change.[58]

> *Pharaoh's chariots and his army He cast into the sea and the elite of his officers sank in the Reed Sea.* (Shemot 15:4)

The death of those who perished in the depths of the sea was more painful than for those who perished by the water's edge. Pharaoh's chariots and army were extremely wicked, and they suffered the more painful death. The elite of Pharaoh's officers believed in God;

---

56. *Tiferet Yehonatan*

57. *Tiferet Yehonatan*

58. *Tiferet Yehonatan*

they were just too frightened to rebel against Pharaoh. God rewarded them by not killing them in the more painful way he killed Pharaoh's army.[59]

Your right hand, God is most powerful; Your right hand, God crushes the enemy. (Shemot 15:6)

The attribute of strict justice complained to God that the Jewish people didn't deserve to be saved because they were idol worshippers. God used the attribute of mercy and compassion, and as a result, the Jewish people were saved.

Why didn't God use the attribute of mercy and save the Egyptians as well? God did, in fact, use the attribute of mercy. However, the Egyptians' sins were so great that even the attribute of mercy was unable to save them. This will explain the double expression in the above quoted verse: "Your right hand, God is most powerful; Your right hand God crushes the enemy." Your right hand, the attribute of mercy, is most powerful in saving the Jewish people. However, your right hand, the attribute of mercy, crushes the enemy because it was unable to save the Egyptians due to their many sins.[60]

And with Your great pride You tear down those who rise up against You; You send forth Your burning wrath; it devours them like straw. (Shemot 15:7)

God judged the Egyptians with the attribute of mercy; nevertheless, they were sentenced to death. In truth, the whole Egyptian nation should have been put to death. However, the attribute of mercy was successful in the sense that only the Egyptians who were by the Reed Sea perished while the rest of the Egyptian nation survived. Based on this, the verse quoted can be understood to mean that if God would have sent forth God's wrath and judged the Egyptians only with the

---

59. *Tiferet Yehonatan*

60. *Tiferet Yehonatan*

attribute of strict justice, it would devour them like straw and the Egyptian nation as a whole would have been destroyed.[61]

> *And with the breath of Your nostrils the waters were heaped up;*
> *the running water stood erect like a wall; the depths congealed*
> *in the heart of the sea.* (Shemot 15:8)

The Egyptians believed that the splitting of the sea was not a miracle, as nature can cause the splitting of a sea. And Moshe knew the exact time when the waters would split; he timed the entry of the Jewish people at that time, resulting in their being saved. The Egyptians entered once the waters had begun to return to their natural flow, which resulted in their drowning.

The above verse clearly proves that the splitting of the sea was miraculous when it states, "the depths congealed in the heart of the sea." Water congealing and turning into hard rock is not a natural occurrence. Rather, what the Jewish people and the Egyptians experienced was a miraculous intervention.

> *You blew with Your wind, the sea covered them; they sank like*
> *lead in the powerful waters.* (Shemot 15:10)

Even though the sea was raging, and in such a situation, a body or object would be tossed around and not sink rapidly, God performed a miracle, and the bodies of the Egyptians sank to the depths as if they were heavy like lead falling to the seabed in calm waters.

The reason God performed this miracle for the Egyptians was to reward them for what Pharaoh had said, as recorded in the previous verse:

> *The enemy said, I will pursue, I will overtake, I will share the*
> *booty; my desire will be filled from them; I will draw my sword,*
> *my hand will impoverish them.* (Shemot 15:9)

---

61. *Tiferet Yehonatan*

The rabbis understood that when Pharaoh said, "I will draw my sword," he was declaring that he would only draw his sword but would not kill the Jewish people. They therefore were rewarded that their bodies sank quickly to the seabed and were not tossed around in the raging waters.[62]

Who is like You among the powerful, O Lord? Who is like You, powerful in the holy place? Too awesome for praises, performing wonders! (Shemot 15:11)

You inclined Your right hand; the earth swallowed them up. (Shemot 15:12)

The word *right* can be understood to mean taking an oath. We can now understand the above verse to mean that God took an oath after the flood. He would never destroy mankind by drowning them in the sea and leaving their corpses to rot in the water as He had done in the times of Noach. God therefore instructed the sea to spit the bodies onto dry land, and "the earth swallowed them up" in order they could be buried in the ground in a respectful manner.[63]

With Your loving kindness You led the people You redeemed; You led them with Your might to Your holy abode. (Shemot 15:13)

God had promised Abraham that "the fourth generation will return to the Land of Israel." The exile began from the time of the birth of Yitzchak. From the birth of Yitzchak until the exodus from Egypt was 400 years. Each generation is 100 years. However, the Jewish people remained in the desert for a further forty years. If that is the case, the Jewish people did not return to Israel at the time of the fourth generation. They returned forty years later.

The Jewish people brought the paschal lamb while still in Egypt.

---

62. *Tiferet Yehonatan*

63. *Tiferet Yehonatan*

The question is posed: How could the Jewish people bring the sacrifice while still in Egypt? The sacrifice could only be brought to the site of the Temple. The commentaries explain: God performed a miracle, and he brought the Jewish people on the wings of eagles to the site of the Temple, and they slaughtered and ate the sacrifice there, and then God returned them to Egypt.

If that is how things unfolded, the Jewish people's forty years in the desert is no longer problematic. God promised Abraham that the fourth generation will return. Indeed, that is what happened. The Jewish people briefly returned at the fourth generation, they then spent forty years in the desert, and at the conclusion of the forty years, the Jewish people entered Israel on a permanent basis.

We can now understand that in the above quoted verse "Your loving kindness" is synonymous with Abraham, and God promised Abraham that the fourth generation would return to Israel. The second half of the verse resolves the question concerning the Jewish people remaining in the desert for another forty years by stating, "You led them with Your might to Your holy abode." The Jewish people did return briefly to "Your holy abode" (the site of the Temple) on the night of the exodus to eat the sacrifice.[64]

A people heard, they trembled; a shudder seized the inhabitants
of Pileshes (Shemot 15:14)

When the Philistines saw that God was taking the Jewish people via the desert and not via Pileshes, the Philistines thought that God was not powerful enough to take the Jewish people via their land. However, after the splitting of the sea, they realized that the reason the Jewish people didn't travel via Pileshes was not because God couldn't defeat the Philistines but rather because God wanted the world to see and hear about the miracle of the splitting of the sea. This realization brought great dread and fear upon the inhabitants of Pileshes.[65]

---

64. *Tiferet Yehonatan*
65. *Tiferet Yehonatan*

Then the chieftains of Edom were startled (Shemot 15:15)

The nation Edom are descendants of Esau, the brother of Ya'akov and the son of Yitzchak. The Edomites felt the blessing of Yitzchak to Ya'akov was not fulfilled; likewise the blessing of God to Ya'akov was similarly not fulfilled. However, when they saw the splitting of the sea, they realized all the blessings were fulfilled, and that is why they were startled.[66]

The powerful men of Moab were seized by trembling
(Shemot 15:15)

Sarah, the wife of Abraham, was seized by King Abimelech (from whom the Moabites descended). The Moabites believed that Sarah was impregnated by Abimelech. And Yitzchak was the son of Abimelech, not the son of Abraham. Therefore, Abraham's blessings would not be bestowed upon the Jewish people but rather upon them, the Moabites.

Likewise, Pharaoh thought the Jewish people born in Egypt were born by illegitimate relationships. He reasoned that if the Egyptians were able to subjugate the Jewish men, they were definitely able to subjugate the Jewish women.

It is well known that someone born by an illegitimate relationship will drown. Pharaoh, therefore, instructed all newborn Jewish boys should be cast into the sea. Since they were all illegitimate, their punishment would be death by drowning.

When the Jewish people were miraculously saved by the splitting of the sea, they realized Yitzchak is the son of Abraham, and the Jewish people are the descendants of Abraham. The Moabites would not be receiving God's or Abraham's blessings; they therefore "were seized by trembling."[67]

All the inhabitants of Canaan melted. (Shemot 15:15)

---

66. *Tiferet Yehonatan*

67. *Tiferet Yehonatan*

The Canaanites were under the impression that the Jewish people would not be inheriting their land since God did not lead the Jewish people via the land of the Philistines. After the splitting of the sea, they realized that God led them via the Reed Sea to show the world His greatness, and they no longer could infer that the Jewish people were not planning to conquer their land. Therefore, the *Canaanites melted*.[68]

May dread and fright fall upon them; with the arm of Your greatness may they become as still as a stone, until Your people cross over, O Lord, until this nation that You have acquired crosses over. (Shemot 15:16)

When Yehoshua brought the Jewish people into the land of Canaan, he informed the Canaanites that if any of them wanted to make peace with the Jewish people, they would be accepted. The Canaanites did not accept Yehoshua's offer. In our verse, we read that the Canaanites were frightened and dreaded the Jewish people. If that is the case, why didn't they embrace Yehoshua's offer?

The answer to this question is alluded to in our verse. The verse reads, while it is true "May dread and fright fall upon them," the Canaanites will fear the Jewish people. They will not agree to make peace with the Jewish people in the times of Yehoshua. As the verse continues "with the arm of Your greatness may they become as still as a stone," God wanted the Jewish people to inherit the Land of Israel. He therefore didn't want the Canaanites to make peace with the Jewish people: "He therefore hardened their hearts to be like a stone."[69]

The Lord will reign for all eternity. When Pharaoh's horses came with his chariots and his horsemen into the sea, and the Lord brought the waters of the sea back upon them, and the children of Israel walked on dry land in the midst of the sea. (Shemot 15:18–19)

---

68. *Tiferet Yehonatan*

69. *Tiferet Yehonatan*

The word *Lord* refers to God's attribute of mercy. The word *reign* refers to God's attribute of strict justice. As Shlomo Hamelech (King Solomon) writes in Mishlei (Proverbs) 29:6:

A king establishes the country with justice.

This verse shows the link between sovereignty and the attribute of strict justice. The above quoted verse impresses upon us that God used the attribute of mercy and strict justice simultaneously.

How do we see this?

The verse says, "and the Lord brought the waters of the sea back upon them, and the children of Israel walked on dry land in the midst of the sea." At the same time, the Jewish people were walking on dry land, the Egyptians were drowning. If each attribute acted at separate times, the Jewish people would have arrived on the other side of the sea (mercy), and then the Egyptians would have drowned (strict justice).[70]

Miriam, the prophetess, Aaron's sister, took a timbrel in her hand, and all the women came out after her with timbrels and with dances. (Shemot 15:20)

The Talmud (Sotah 12b) asks: Why does the verse say that Miriam was the sister of Aaron? Wasn't she also the sister of Moshe?

It is well known that when Moshe was born, all prophecies were via Moshe. After Moshe's birth, all prophets (including Miriam) lost the ability to prophesize.

The above verse can be understood to mean that Miriam *was* a prophetess. She had the ability to prophesize when she was *Aaron's sister*. Once her younger brother Moshe was born, she no longer had the ability to prophesize; instead, she "took a timbrel in her hand."[71]

It is interesting to note that when Moshe and the men sang their song, they did not use any musical instruments. Why did Miriam and

---

70. *Tiferet Yehonatan*

71. *Tiferet Yehonatan*

the women use musical instruments? The Talmud (Pesachim 116a) teaches that one can only be a conduit for God's prophecy if one is in a state of *simcha* (happiness and joy). By the exodus, the men were on a very high spiritual level, and they did not need a musical instrument to be a conduit for God's prophecy. The women, however, needed to be imbued with *simcha* prior to their being able to prophesize. Therefore, the men didn't need to use musical instruments but the women did.

Another reason the women used a musical instrument can be suggested. The Talmud (Berachot 24a) teaches us that men are prohibited from hearing women sing. The women used a musical instrument to ensure that the men would not be able to hear them when they sang their song.[72]

Why did the women specifically use the timbrel? The Ibn Ezra writes that there are ten spheres, and each sphere is symbolized by a musical instrument. The Egyptians worshiped the sun, and the musical instrument of the sun is the timbrel. The women wanted to use the timbrel to demonstrate that the god of the Egyptians was unable to save them.[73]

> *And Miriam called out to them. Sing to the Lord for He is very exalted; a horse and its rider He cast into the sea.* (Shemot 15:21)

It is interesting to note that when the men sang, they praised God for two things: for saving them and for destroying the enemy, while the women only praised God for destroying the enemy; they did not praise God for saving their lives. Why didn't the women thank God for saving their lives? You would imagine being saved is of greater significance than the destruction of their enemy.

The Talmud (Sotah 11a) states that it was in the merit of the righteous women the Jewish people were redeemed from Egypt, implying that the men in their own right were not worthy of being saved. The

---

72. *Tiferet Yehonatan*

73. *Tiferet Yehonatan*

fact they were saved was a miracle. Therefore, the men had to thank God for being saved as well.

The women who were righteous deserved to be saved. They therefore didn't need to praise God for being saved. However, they did need to praise God for the destruction of the Egyptians.[74]

In the above verse, the verb *sing* is written in the plural, attesting to the fact that all the women sang. By the men, however, the verb for singing is *ashirah* (I will sing), implying that only one person sang, that being Moshe.

Why the distinction?

King Chizkiyahu did not sing songs of praise to God when his enemy Sancheriv was destroyed. The reason given is because King Chizkiyahu was saved in the merit of King David. This implies that one should only sing songs of praise to God if you merit the miracle in your own right.

The Jewish men lacked faith in God, and they didn't believe God would redeem them. The waters split in the merit of Moshe. Therefore, when the men sang a song of praise, they could not include themselves in the song. They therefore said, "I will sing," referring to Moshe.

The women had great faith in God and believed God would redeem them. The Talmud (Sotah 11a) states that it was in the merit of the righteous women the Jewish people were redeemed from Egypt. They therefore were able to say, "We will all sing a song of praise to God," since it was in the merit of the women that the Jewish women were saved.[75]

---

74. *Tiferet Yehonatan*

75. *Tiferet Yehonatan*

Shavuot

A Discussion Between God and the Angels

The rabbis bring up an interesting discussion between God and the angels concerning the giving of the Torah:

The angels said to God, "The Torah should remain in heaven."

God responded, "The Torah discusses what a person is permitted and prohibited in doing. The angels are not capable in fulfilling the laws."

The angels questioned God's answer: "The Torah discusses the laws needed to be fulfilled by the Cohanim and Leviim, and how will they be able to fulfill them?"

God responded, "When the Temple is built, the Cohen and the Levite will be able to fulfill these commandments."

This discussion between God and the angels is alluded to in Tehillim (Psalms) 29:11:

> The Lord shall grant strength to His people;
> the Lord shall bless His people with peace.

The word *strength* refers to the Torah: "The Lord shall grant strength to His people." When God gave the Torah to the Jewish people on Mount Sinai, He gave them strength. The angels asked God, "How could God give the Torah to the Jewish people? The Cohanim and Leviim would be unable to fulfill their commandments."

God's answer is contained in the second part of the verse: "the Lord shall bless His people with peace." True peace is when the Temple is built. God answers the angels that the Cohanim and Leviim will fulfill their commandments when there is *peace*, when the Temple is built.[76]

---

76. *Midrash Yehonatan*

Moshe and the Angels

The Talmud (Shabbat 88b) records a discussion between God and the angels. The angels requested that the Torah remain in heaven. God asked Moshe to respond to the angels' request. Moshe said to the angels, "The Torah obligates the Jewish people to keep Shabbat, something that you cannot do."

This conversation between God, the angels, and Moshe will explain why the Torah wrote two verses in close proximity one to the other. The Torah states:

Moshe was on the mountain for forty days. (Shemot 24:18)

The Torah further states:

Moshe gathered the Jewish people . . . and on the seventh day it shall be a holy day a day of rest for God (Shemot 35: 1–2)

Moshe was on the mountain receiving the Torah. During that time, he justified why the Jewish people and not the angels should receive the Torah: because the Jewish people could observe the Shabbat. That explains why soon after descending the mountain, he taught the Jewish people the laws of Shabbat. Hence, the two sections are written in close proximity in the Torah.

And he took the Book of the Covenant and read it within the hearing of the people, and they said, "All that the Lord spoke we will do and we will listen." (Shemot 24:7)

The Yalkut Shimoni (rabbinic commentary) in Yitro 279 states that the book of the covenant refers to Sefer Bereishit (Book of Genesis). After the Jewish people heard Sefer Bereishit, they responded, "We will do and we will listen."

Why specifically did Moshe read Bereishit? Secondly, why after hearing Bereishit did the Jewish people respond by saying, "We will do and we will listen"?

The Talmud (Sotah 5a) states that the Torah was given on Mount Sinai, the smallest of all the mountains. This impresses upon us that one needs to be humble when it comes to the study of the Torah.

In Bereishit, we learn about creation. By the creation of man God said, "Let us make man." The rabbis ask, "Who is God referring to when He says *us?*" They answer that it refers to the heavenly court. God consulted with the heavenly court if He should create man.

In Rashi's commentary on this verse, he writes that since God sought the advice of the heavenly court, similarly when deciding a court case, the senior judge should seek the opinion of the more junior judges before rendering his decision. This demonstrates God's humility.

We will now be able to answer our original two questions.

Moshe wanted to impress upon the Jewish people the importance of having humility. After Moshe read the Jewish people Bereishit, they became aware of how important it is to be humble as seen by God's actions when he created man. By immediately responding, "We will do," the Jewish people were demonstrating how humble they were. The Jewish people were willing to do everything they would be instructed in.

God Gave the Torah via Moshe

The Midrash states that God sustains the Jewish people in the merit of their *emunah* (faith) in Him. Why specifically is the mitzvah of faith in God singled out? What about all the other mitzvot the Jewish people fulfill?

In numerous places, the rabbis state that God fulfills all of the 613 commandments the Jewish people are commanded to fulfill.

The Torah states:

> One is prohibited to withhold the wages of one's worker, as it says, "The wage of a hired worker shall not stay overnight with you until morning." (Vayikra 19:13)

The Talmud (Kiddushin 39b) states that the Jewish people are to receive their reward for fulfilling God's commandments in *Olam HaBa* (the world to come). If God fulfills all the commandments, He needs to reward the Jews in this world and not wait till the Jew enters the world to come—just as the householder needs to pay his day worker at the end of the day.

We can answer this question based on the Talmud (Bava Metzia 111a). The Talmud sets forth the following law: If a householder appoints an agent to hire workers and the agent tells the workers the householder will be paying the workers for their work, the agent and the householder are not obligated to pay the workers at the conclusion of the day's work. The agent is not liable since the work was not done for him and he told the workers the householder would pay them. The householder is not liable since he didn't hire the workers himself.

God gave the Torah to the Jewish people via Moshe, His agent. In Bava Metzia, the Talmud taught us that if you hire workers via an agent, you don't have to pay the workers at the end of the day's work. That being the case, God does not have to reward His people in this world since they were given the laws via Moshe.

However, the Talmud (Makkot 24a) states that the Jewish people heard the first two commandments directly from God: "I am the Lord Your God who took you out of Egypt" and the second commandment "You shall have no other God." That being the case, God would be obligated to reward the Jewish people in this world since these two commandments were heard directly from God and not via Moshe, His agent.

We now understand the Midrash quoted at the beginning of this section. The Midrash said, "The Jewish people are sustained in this world due to their faith in God." The question posed was, why specifically faith?

The commandment of having faith in God (which is based on the first two of the Ten Commandments) was the only commandment the Jews heard directly from God, and as a result, they needed to be rewarded in this world for it.[77]

---

77. *Midrash Yehonatan*

The Covenant

And He told you His covenant, which He commanded you to do, the Ten Commandments, and He inscribed them on two stone tablets. (Devarim 4:13)

Concerning the Ten Commandments, what was the covenant between God and the Jewish People?

King David writes in Tehillim (Psalms) 94:17:

Had the Lord not been my help, in an instant my soul would rest silent.

King David is telling us that without God's help, we would not be able to defeat the *Yetzer Hara*—the evil inclination.

The Ten Commandments are divided into two categories: The first five are commandments between man and God. They include the obligation to believe in God and not to serve idols. These commandments are seemingly not beneficial for mankind and man would not be driven to fulfill them on his own. The second five are between man and his fellow man. These include the prohibition of murder and of kidnapping. The second five in contrast to the first five are beneficial for mankind, and the human being would see the benefit in fulfilling them.

We will now be able to understand the covenant as it relates to the Ten Commandments. God made a covenant with the Jewish people, if you fulfill the last five commandments which are not so challenging, I will help you in fulfilling the first five commandments that are more challenging to fulfill.

Bein Hametzarim

DURING THE THREE WEEKS BETWEEN THE 17TH OF TAAMUZ and Tisha B'Av (Bein Hametzarim), we say three special Haftorahs. The first week, we say *Divrei Yermiyahu* (the words of the Prophet Jeremiah). The second week we say *Shimu dvar Hashem* (listen to the word of God), and the final Haftorah is *Chazon Yeshayahu* (the vision of the Prophet Isaiah). The Jewish people sinned by what they said, what they heard, and what they saw. Therefore, the Haftorahs begin with the themes of speaking, hearing, and seeing.[78]

---

78. *Ahavat Yehonatan*

Tisha B'Av

Note: Tisha B'Av is the 9th of Av. The first and second Temple were destroyed on this day.

Chaggai Hanavi (Haggai the Prophet) writes:

The glory of this last House shall be greater than the first one.
(Haggai 2:9)

The Talmud (Bava Batra 3a) teaches that the first and last House refers to the first and second Temple. The third and final Temple would be so much more superior that we would not be able to compare it to the previous two Temples.

In what way was the second Temple superior to the first? The first Temple's greatness remained somewhat hidden to the other nations. We don't read that foreign kings and leaders sent gifts and sacrifices to the Temple, unlike the second Temple, where we read that the nations of the world and their kings honored the Temple by sending it gifts and sacrifices.

Yermiyahu Hanavi (Jeremiah the Prophet) alludes to the destruction of both Temples in Eichah (Lamentation). In the opening verse of Eichah, he writes:

O How has the city that was once so populous remained lonely! She has become like a widow. She that was great amongst the nations, a princess amongst the provinces, has become tributary.

In the first half of the verse, the prophet is referring to the first Temple. He therefore says, "O How has the city that was once so populous," meaning it was heavily populated with Jewish people; however, visitors did not populate it. The verse continues and says, "[The Temple] remained lonely." After the destruction of the first Temple, there remained no inhabitants in Jerusalem. As the Talmud (Shabbat 145b) states, after the destruction of the first Temple, for the next fifty-two years, no one traveled throughout the land of Yehudah, the site of the first Temple. The verse then continues, "She has become like a widow"—like a widow but not really a widow, meaning she will remain a widow for only a short amount of time, since the Jewish people knew they would be exiled for only seventy years.

The second part of the verse refers to the destruction of the second Temple. The verse continues, "She that was great amongst the nations, a princess amongst the provinces." During the period of the second Temple, the temple was revered by the nations of the world. The verse doesn't repeat the statement "remained lonely" after the destruction of the second Temple, since the Jewish people remained living in Israel. The verse continues and says, "has become tributary," meaning the Jewish people living in Israel had to pay taxes to the Roman Empire.

Hate without Cause

The Talmud (Yoma 9b) explains that the reason the second Temple was destroyed was because of *sinat chinam* (hate without cause) among the Jewish people. Why was this sin singled out as the cause of the destruction? Unfortunately, the Jewish people had transgressed many other sins. The Tzedokim were the Sadducees, a large group of Jewish people who did not believe in the oral tradition; their many sins were sufficient grounds to destroy the Temple.

At the time of the destruction of the second Temple, many great rabbis lived, such as Rabbi Yochanan ben Zakkai and his colleagues. Their greatness would have been sufficient to protect the Jewish people and the Temple from being destroyed. However, since the Jewish people were not living in harmony with one another and there was hatred among the Jewish people, these great rabbis could no longer protect the Jewish people and the Temple from being destroyed.

This thought is alluded to in the Midrash. The Midrash quotes the words of the Navi Yeshaya (the Prophet Isaiah):

You were sold for nothing and you will be redeemed for nothing.
(Yeshayahu 52:3)

The word for *nothing* is *chinam*. "You were sold for nothing" means that you were sold because of *sinat chinam* (hate without cause). And you will be redeemed because of *ahavat chinam*—love for your fellow Jew—which will be based on no real cause.[79]

The Temple's Curtains

The Talmud (Gittin 56b) states that when the *parochos* (the curtain in the Temple) was pierced, blood flowed from the curtain. The Romans falsely believed that they had killed the Creator, God forbid. A question can be asked: Why did God perform a miracle that led to such an error?

The curtain was placed in close proximity to where the altar was placed, and when the Cohen sprinkled the blood on the altar, some of the blood landed on the curtain. All of the blood miraculously was absorbed into the curtain. Once the curtain was pierced, the blood that was absorbed into the curtain became impure. The impure blood could no longer remain miraculously absorbed in the curtain, and the blood flowed from the curtain.

Initially, when one learns this section of Talmud, it would seem that the blood flowing from the curtain was miraculous. The new explanation is that the miracle was the constant absorbing of the blood into the curtain. The blood flowing wasn't a miracle; it was the natural result of the removal of the miracle that allowed the blood to be absorbed into the curtain.

---

79. *Ahavat Yehonatan*

Fifteenth of Av

Note: As a result of the sin of the spies, the Jewish people wandered in the desert for the next forty years. During those years, the generation that left Egypt perished.

The Talmud (Bava Batra 121b) states that on the fifteenth of Av of the year the Jewish people entered Israel, God resumed communicating with Moshe.

Tosafot explains that the Jewish people ceased to pass away on the ninth of Av and the days of mourning concluded on the fifteenth of Av. God did not speak to Moshe until the days of mourning had passed.

The following is posed: Aaron, the High Priest, passed away on the first day of Av of the year the Jewish people entered Israel. The Torah states:

> *The Jewish people mourned Aaron for thirty days.*
> (Bamidbar 20:29)

Why did God speak to Moshe on the fifteenth of Av? True, the mourning for those who perished due to the sin of the spies had concluded; however, the Jewish people were still mourning the passing of Aaron for another fourteen days.

When the Jewish people are mourning here on earth, God is in mourning in heaven. This idea is seen in Rashi's explanation of the phrase, "and He became grieved in His heart." With regard to the story of the flood (Bereishit 6:6), Rashi explains that God *mourned* over the destruction of His handiwork. Similarly, when man is suffering, God is suffering as well. This idea is seen in the Talmud (Hagigah 15b) where it states that when man is suffering, God says, "My head is heavy my arm is heavy." Therefore, when heaven is in a state of mourning, God doesn't communicate with mankind.

When mankind is mourning the passing of a *tzaddik* (righteous individual) such as Aaron, heaven isn't in a state of mourning, as heaven is rejoicing that the tzaddik is returning home.

Once the mourning for those who passed away due to the sin of the spies, God also concluded His state of mourning. The mourning for Aaron on earth did not cause there to be a state of mourning in heaven since Aaron was a tzaddik. Therefore, God was able to resume communication with Moshe on the fifteenth of Av.

Beit Hamikdash

Note: The Temple was not constructed on Shabbat.

After the Torah instructs the Jewish people to build the Tabernacle, the Torah states, "You shall guard My Shabbat." The question is posed: Why was it necessary to repeat the obligation of keeping the Shabbat and repeating it next to the section that deals with the construction of the Tabernacle?

The Midrash explains that God repeated the obligation to keep Shabbat and placed it next to the laws of building the Tabernacle for the sake of Moshe. The Midrash needs to be understood: Why specifically for Moshe? In what way was Moshe unique that he needed to hear the laws of Shabbat again and the rest of the Jewish people did not?

The Talmud (Yevamot 6a) discusses whether or not the Jewish people were allowed to build the Temple on Shabbat. The Talmud says that one may not and bases its ruling on the verse "My Shabbat you shall observe."

A question can be posed: Why do I need a verse to teach that one may not build the Temple on Shabbat? The rule is that if I need to fulfill a positive commandment and the only way I can fulfill the positive commandment is by transgressing both a positive and negative commandment, the law is that I am not permitted to fulfill the positive commandment.

The building of the Temple is a positive commandment. If one works on the Shabbat, one transgresses both a positive and negative commandment. Based on the rule above, one wouldn't be able to build the Temple on Shabbat. If this is the case, why do I need a specific verse to teach me that one can't build the Temple on Shabbat when it can be derived from the above rule?

We find a similar situation when a positive commandment clashes with both a positive and negative commandment. And, in that case (unlike what is mentioned earlier), the positive commandment takes precedence over the positive and negative commandment.

To prepare the *parah adumah* (red heifer) is a positive commandment. A Cohen must ensure that he remains in a state of purity; if he doesn't, he transgresses both a positive and negative commandment. The law is that anyone involved in preparing the red heifer becomes impure.

If a person becomes impure, how can the Cohen be involved in purifying the red heifer? True, the Cohen will be fulfilling a positive commandment; however, at the same time, he will be transgressing a positive and a negative commandment.

The case of the red heifer is unique and therefore the general rule that a positive commandment is pushed aside when it is confronted by a positive and negative commandment does not apply. The reason it is unique is because the Torah, by the laws of the red heifer, uses the words:

This is the statute of the Torah (Bamidbar 19:2)

A *statute* refers to those commandments that are beyond human understanding; therefore, no other laws of the Torah could be learned from it.

The Midrash (Bamidbar Rabah 19:2) states that even though God concealed the reason for the red heifer from the Jewish people, He did reveal the reason to Moshe. If that is the case, for Moshe, the laws of the red heifer are not unique, and one could use the laws of the red heifer to be the basis for other laws to be learned from it. We could then learn the following: Just as the Cohen can be involved in the process of preparing the red heifer (even though it is a positive commandment up against a negative and positive commandment), likewise Moshe should be able to build the Tabernacle on Shabbat (even though it is a positive commandment up against a negative and positive commandment) since, in Moshe's case, we will be able to compare the laws of Shabbat to the laws of the red heifer.

The reason why this is applicable only to Moshe is because, as said above, Moshe knew the reason for the red heifer; it was no longer a statute and therefore no longer a unique law.

That is why the Midrash said that the verse "you shall guard My Shabbat" from which we learned the prohibition of building the Temple was said to Moshe specifically, since otherwise he would have learned that he could build the Temple based on its comparison to the laws of the red heifer. The Jewish people did not know the reason for the red heifer. The laws of the red heifer remained a statute, and no law could be learned from it. They therefore would have been able to deduce the prohibition of building the Temple on Shabbat based on the principle that a positive commandment (building the Temple) does not push aside the positive and negative commandment of not desecrating the Shabbat.

The Site of the Temple Was Created Last

Note: In this next section we are introduced to a process of Talmudic logic and reasoning. We will be presented with three arguments. Seemingly each argument is independent of the other. However, what Reb Yehonatan attempts to do is show how all three arguments can be linked together and depending on which opinion you accept in one of the arguments will impact which opinion you will need to follow in the other two arguments.

> *Yitro (the father in law of Moshe) heard, and as a result he traveled to meet up with his son in law and the rest of the Jewish people. (Shemot 18:1)*

The Mekhilta, a book written by Rabbi Yishmael, wonders what Yitro heard that convinced him to travel and meet the Jewish people. The Mekhilta answers that he heard the great miracle of the splitting of the sea. Why was the miracle of the splitting of the sea so compelling that Yitro left Midian and traveled to the desert to meet up with the Jewish people?

God has many names. Each name speaks of a specific quality or trait that God is using at that moment in time. For example:

The name *Yud-Hei-Vov-Hei* speaks of God's compassion and kindness.

The name *Elo-him* speaks of God's attribute of strict justice.

The name *Sha-dai* speaks of God's attribute of curtailing or halting a given process.

There is an argument among the rabbinic commentaries when God needed to express Himself with the name *Sha-dai*. One opinion is that when God created the world, He created the world from a center point and began to expand. The world continued to expand, and God had to tell the world, *Sha-dai*—it is sufficient; the world doesn't need to expand any further. Another opinion is that God said, I am He whose Godliness suffices for every creature.

The Talmud (Yoma 54b) records an argument about how the world was created. One opinion is that the world was created from its epicenter and continued to expand. The epicenter was the site of the Temple. This approach leads us to the understanding that the site of the Temple was created first. The other opinion is that the world was created from its extremities and the world grew inward until the four sides met. This approach leads us to the understanding that the site of the Temple was created last.

In terms of creation, do we say that what was created first is more important than that which was created after it or that which was created last is superior to that which proceeded it in the creation process?

Recognizing the significance of the site of the Temple, the answer to the above question will be dependent on how the world was created.

According to the opinion that the world expanded, the Temple site was created first. This opinion will be of the view that what is created earlier during the six days of creation is of greater significance. According to the opinion that the world was created from its extremities, the Temple site was created last. This opinion will be of the view that what is created last or later during the six days of creation is of more significance.

The Midrash (Shemot Rabbah 21:6) relates that when Moshe came to the Reed Sea and commanded it to split, the sea responded, "I was created on the third day and you (mankind) were created on the sixth day. I am therefore more significant than you, and I don't need to follow your instructions and I don't need to split."

The waters did, in fact, split. The argument of the sea was not accepted. This proves that what is created last is of more significance and the waters had to listen to Moshe. If that which is created last is of more importance, we are forced to say the world was created from its extremities, and the site of the Temple was created last.

That being the case, God did not have to tell the world *Sha-dai*— stop expanding since the world was created inward. Rather God said, *Sha-dai*. I am He whose Godliness suffices for every creature.

Bearing all this in mind, we will now understand why after hearing of the splitting of the sea Yitro came to meet the Jewish people. Yitro now understood the following three points:

1. What is created last is more important. (The waters had to split as Moshe was created last.)

2. The Temple was created last. (The world was created at its extremities.)

3. God used the name *Sha-dai* to impress upon the world that His Godliness is sufficient and there is no need to serve idols.

Yitro now understood that he needed to abandon his life of idol worship and embrace God Himself.

The Menorah Was Lit Only at Night

Aaron and his sons shall set it (the Menorah – candelabra) up before the Lord from evening till morning; (it shall be) an everlasting statute for their generations, from the children of Israel. (Shemot 27:21)

The Torah is teaching us that the menorah was only lit during the duration of the night. The menorah did not burn during the day. When the Temple existed, where there were windows and no roof, there was no need for the menorah to burn during the day. However, the Tabernacle had no windows and had a roof. The Tabernacle was dark during the day as well. One may have thought the menorah should be lit during the day as well. Therefore, the Torah states, "(it shall be) an everlasting statute for their generations," to impress upon us that the menorah was only lit at night both in the Temple and in the Tabernacle.[80]

Why Was Deborah a Prophetess?

Deborah was a prophetess, she was the wife of Lapidus. (Shoftim 4:4)

The Midrash explains the word *lapid* can be translated to mean a flame. The verse has two parts to it. The first part was that Deborah was a prophetess and the second part was that she was married to Lapidus. The verse should be read backward—the second part before the first part: "She was the wife of Lapidus (a flame)," meaning that she was very connected to the menorah, which had seven flames burning from it.

In what way was she connected?

She made wicks for it. Therefore, she merited in becoming,

---

80. *Tiferet Yehonatan*

"Deborah was a prophetess." Why by making wicks did she merit becoming a prophetess?

One of the reasons we were instructed to light the menorah is so that the glory of God would permeate the Temple. If we did not light the menorah, the Cohen would be able to see where he was going by seeing via God's glory. This would be considered disrespectful. By lighting the menorah, the Cohen would navigate where he was going by using the lights of the menorah.

Deborah made extremely thick wicks, thereby ensuring the Cohen would definitely not need to use the light of God's glory. Since Deborah honored God in such a manner, she merited having God's glory descend upon her. She therefore merited becoming a prophetess.

The Temple: An Expression of God's Humility

The Talmud (Megillah 31a) states that wherever the Torah mentions God's greatness it also mentions God's humility. This is evident when we speak of the Temple. On the one hand, the Prophet Yeshayahu (Prophet Isaiah) writes:

> *So says the Lord, The heavens are My throne, and the earth is My footstool; the whole world is filled with God's glory.*
> (Yeshayahu 66:1)

Even so, God instructed the Jewish people to build a small structure where God's glory would be found. Likewise, God chose the Jewish people since they were small in number, as the Torah writes:

> *For you are the least of all the peoples.* (Devarim 7:7)

Similarly, God's presence rests on the downtrodden as the Prophet Yeshayahu writes:

> *But to this one will I look, to one poor and of crushed spirit, who hastens to do my bidding.* (Yeshayahu 66:2)

First and Second Temple

On the Laws of Beit Habechirah 6:16, Rambam states that the sanctity of the first Temple left the Temple when it was destroyed. The sanctity of the second Temple remained even after the Temple was destroyed. Why the distinction?

The Prophet Yermiyahu writes:

> Our heritage has been turned over to strangers,
> our houses to aliens. (Eichah 5:2)

Likewise, the Prophet Yeshayahu writes:

> Our sanctuary and our glory, wherein our forefathers
> praised You, is burnt with fire. (Yeshayahu 64:10)

Both prophets are referring to the first Temple, and they both refer to the Temple as being ours, our inheritance.

In Tehillim (Psalms) 79:1, it is written:

> A song of Asaph. O God! Nations have come into Your heritage,
> they have defiled Your Holy Temple.

Asaph is referring to the second Temple, and he refers to the Temple as being God's inheritance.

Since the first Temple is man's inheritance and man is not eternal, likewise man's inheritance, the first Temple, is not eternal. However, the second Temple is God's inheritance. Just as God is eternal, so is the sanctity of the second Temple.[81]

---

81. *Yaaroth Devash*

Difference Between First and Second Temple

The Prophet Chaggai writes:

> *The glory of this last House shall be greater than the first one,*
> *said the Lord of Hosts.* (Chaggai 2:9)

This can be understood to mean the following: During the period of the first Temple, non-Jewish people did not travel to the Land of Israel. They therefore did not see and experience God's miracles emanating from the Temple. However, during the period of the second Temple, non-Jewish people did travel to the Temple and saw the wonders of God, and they too believed in Him. We see this idea expressed in the writings of the Prophet Yechezkel. The prophet writes:

> *So says the Lord God: When I gather in the house of Israel*
> *from the people among whom they have been scattered, and I*
> *have been sanctified through them in the eyes of the nations.*
> (Yechezkel 28:25)

Yechezkel is referring to the second Temple, and he says the nations of the world will honor Him.

Galut (Exile)

THE NON-BELIEVERS WERE MOCKING THE JEWISH PEOPLE and they said to the Jewish people, the first Temple was destroyed because the Jewish people transgressed the three cardinal transgressions: idol worship, illicit relationships, and murder. The Jewish people returned back from exile after only seventy years. The second Temple was destroyed for baseless hate between one another. Seemingly, this transgression is not as severe as the three cardinal sins. Yet, the Jewish people are still in exile.

The non-believers made a drastic mistake. They were under the impression that when the Jewish people returned after the exile of the first Temple, the sins that led to the destruction of the first Temple had been forgiven. This was not the case. God saw that the Jewish people, during the seventy years of the first exile, were separating themselves more and more from God and His Torah. There was a great fear that if they would remain any longer in exile, the Jewish people would totally assimilate with the non-Jewish world, and His Torah would be totally forgotten.

God had no choice, and He had to take them out of exile after seventy years. However, the sins that led to the destruction of the first Temple had not been fully forgiven. Therefore, the present exile is an atonement, not just for unwanted hate between one Jew and another, it is an atonement for the three cardinal sins as well.[82]

---

82. *Yaaroth Devash*

Few in Number

The Talmud (Pesachim 64b) quotes the verse from the Prophet Chaggai:

The glory of this last House shall be greater than the first one, said the Lord of Hosts. (Chaggai 2:9)

The Talmud explains the verse to mean that there were more Jewish people during the period of the second Temple than during the period of the first Temple. Why was this the case?

The family of Kehot were instructed to carry the Holy Ark. The family of Kehot were few in number. One of the explanations given is since the family of Kehot were in such close proximity to the Holy Ark, they were judged more severely. The Talmud (Sukkah 45b) writes that Rabbi Shimon bar Yochai said, "I have seen that people of great stature are few in number." This statement can be understood to mean that people who have the Divine Presence resting upon them are few in number.

During the period of the first Temple, God's presence was present in the Temple. Therefore, the Jewish people were judged more severely, and as a result, they were few in number. During the period of the second Temple, God's presence was not in the Temple. The Jewish people were not judged so severely; therefore, the Jewish people were more in number.[83]

Sulfur and Salt

Sulfur and salt have burned up its entire land. It cannot be sown, nor can it grow [anything]. And all the nations will say, Why did the Lord do so to this land? What is the reason for this great rage of fury? Then they will say, it is because they abandoned the covenant of the Lord. (Devarim 29:22–23)

---

83. *Ahavat Yehonatan*

The Jewish people had sinned, and they needed to be punished. The nations of the world couldn't understand why the land also had to be destroyed.

The Land of Israel is the holiest land in the whole world. When the Jewish people lived there, the land was blessed. However, when the Jewish people were sent into exile, the land couldn't bear being occupied by foreign nations as it couldn't tolerate any form of impurity. Therefore, the Torah writes, "Sulfur and salt have burned up its entire land."

This idea is seen in the writings of Ramban. In a letter written to his son, he says that which is holier, its destruction is more severe. The land of Yehudah is holier than the land of the Galil. Therefore, the destruction in Yehudah was more severe than it was in the Galil. Likewise, Jerusalem was holier than the land of Yehudah. Therefore, its destruction was the most severe.

Jerusalem

The holier a city is, the more it will reflect the level of love between the inhabitants of that city. Jerusalem was the holiest city in Israel; therefore, the love between the people was very strong, as it says in Ethics of the Fathers 5:5, no one ever said to their friend I feel cramped in Jerusalem.

The Land Was Forsaken

The Talmud (Nedarim 81a) records a conversation between God and the leaders of the Jewish people. God asked the Torah scholars and then He asked the prophets, "Why was the Land of Israel destroyed?" The scholars and the prophets were unable to answer God's question. Finally God answered the question, "Because you have forsaken my Torah."

Why were the scholars and prophets unable to answer God's question?

The answer is clearly written in the Torah and is recited twice a day in the Shema. The Torah states:

Beware, lest your heart be misled, and you turn away and worship strange gods and prostrate yourselves before them… and you will perish quickly from upon the good land that the Lord gives you. (Devarim 11: 16–17)

The scholars and the prophets understood God's question to be referring to the actual land itself, as God had asked, "Why was the *land* destroyed?" God didn't ask why the Jewish people were destroyed and sent into exile. They knew why the Jewish people were driven out of the land; the Torah spells it out clearly. What they couldn't understand was why the actual land was punished. God's answer was, "For you have forsaken My Torah."

How does this answer explain why the actual land was destroyed?

The Talmud (Ketubot 112b) states that the Land of Israel is called the land of the deer. The Talmud explains why it is called the land of the deer. The skin of the deer covers the flesh of the animal. However, when it is removed from the deer, it shrivels and the skin can no longer be reattached and cover the flesh of the deer.

Likewise, when the Jewish people lived in Israel, the land was able to contain within it the Jewish people. When they were banished from the land, the land shriveled and it would no longer be large enough to contain within it the Jewish people.

The Torah is God's wisdom and is therefore infinite. The more one studies the Torah, the more one is able to grasp it. If, however, one doesn't study the Torah, his mind in a sense shrivels and will not be able to comprehend the Torah.

We will now be able to comprehend God's response. God answered, "Do you know why the Land of Israel was destroyed in the sense that the land shriveled and would no longer be able to contain within it the Jewish people? Because they have forsaken My Torah." This means that in the same way the human mind will shrivel and will not be able to comprehend God's wisdom if it doesn't study God's Torah, so too the Land of Israel will shrivel and will be unable to contain within it the Jewish people.

From the North

And the word of the Lord came to me a second time, saying:
What do you see? And I said, "I see a bubbling pot, whose foam
is toward the north." (Yermiyahu 1:13)

When the prophet said, "the Lord came to me a second time," this is
alluding to the destruction of the second Temple. One of the reasons
the second Temple was destroyed was because the Jewish people had
accumulated great wealth through illegal means—by charging interest
on loans and by stealing.

The word *north* alludes to wealth as the Talmud (Bava Batra
25b) states that he who desires wealth should turn to the north when
praying. And the Talmud also says, the north wind makes gold flow.
Therefore, the prophet writes, "whose foam is to the north." This is
teaching us that the second Temple was destroyed because the Jewish
people acquired wealth through illegal means.[84]

When Is the End?

The Talmud (Yoma 9b) states that prior to the destruction of the first
Temple, the leaders of the Jewish people revealed to the Jewish people
the gravity of their sins and how their sinning will lead to the destruction of the Temple. Just as the prophets revealed to the Jewish people
what sins they needed to eradicate, the prophets also revealed to the
Jewish people how long they would remain in exile. However, prior to
the destruction of the second Temple, the prophets did not inform the
Jewish people which of their sins would lead to the destruction of the
Temple. They also did not inform the Jewish people when the exile
would end.[85]

---

84. *Ahavat Yehonatan*

85. *Ahavat Yehonatan*

They Failed to Rebuke

The leaders of the Jewish people were obligated to inform the people which sins they needed to do *teshuvah* (repent) for. The reason they were obligated to do so is because if they would have rebuked them, the people would have done teshuvah. Since they didn't rebuke them, the leaders were punished with the same punishment given to the people. This is alluded to by Yermiyahu 1:14, in which he writes:

> *From the north the misfortune will break forth upon all the inhabitants of the land.*

The Hebrew word for *north* is *tzafon*. The word *tzafon* also means hidden. The verse can then be translated to mean, "from the north— from the fact that the leaders concealed from the people their sins, this will result in the punishment of all the inhabitants of the land." The phrase "all the inhabitants" is to include not only the actual sinners but also the leaders who failed to rebuke the people.[86]

The Jewish People of the Diaspora

More than double the population of Jewish people living in Israel lived in the diaspora at the time of the destruction of the second Temple. The reason for this was, since the Jewish people living in Israel had baseless hatred one for the other and they spoke ill about each other, many Jewish people fled Israel and lived in the diaspora.[87]

Prophecy Given to Fools and Children

The Talmud (Bava Batra 12b) states that after the destruction of the Temple, God no longer spoke to the prophets; rather, He bestowed prophecy upon fools and children.

---

86. *Ahavat Yehonatan*

87. *Yaaroth Devash*

This statement can be understood based upon another statement of the Talmud. The Talmud (Rosh Hashanah 17b) states that if the Jewish people on Rosh Hashanah were righteous, God would bless them with an abundance of rain. What would happen if after Rosh Hashanah they sinned and they no longer were worthy of receiving the blessing of an abundance of rain?

God would not remove His blessing of rain; rather, instead of the rain falling on the fields that needed the rain for the crops, He would cause the rain to fall on the mountains and so on where the rain would not be of any benefit for mankind.

Similarly, when the Jewish people were following God's commands, then God would imbue the righteous with His prophecies. However, when the Jewish people were not worthy, He wouldn't curtail His prophecies. Rather, He would share the prophecies with the fools and with the young, which would be of no benefit for the Jewish people.

God Is Present

God said to Shlomo Hamelech (King Solomon):

> *(Concerning) this house which you are building, if you walk in My statutes, and execute My ordinances, and keep all My commandments to walk in them; then will I establish My word with you, which I spoke to David your father.* (Melachim I 6:12)

Through prophecy, God informed King Solomon that if the Jewish people would follow the path of God, then God's presence would forever remain within the Temple. One may be under the impression that if even one Jew will transgress, God will remove His presence from the Temple. Therefore, in the very next verse, God says to King Solomon:

> *And I will dwell among the children of Israel, and will not forsake, My people Israel.* (Melachim I 6:13)

God promises that He will always dwell among the Jewish people and never forsake the Jewish people. And even if the Temple would be destroyed, King Solomon writes in Shir Hashirim 2:9:

He is standing behind our wall, looking from the windows,
peering from the lattices.

This implies that God is always watching.

God's Complete Name

The Talmud (Eruvin 18b) states that from the day the Temple was destroyed, it is sufficient for God to only use two letters of His name. (God's name comprises four letters: *Yud-Hei-Vov-Hei.*) When God uses all four letters, his presence is felt in the world in a revealed manner. For example, the ten plagues in Egypt, the splitting of the sea, or the miracles during the times of the judges, the prophets, and the period of the first Temple. However, when God uses only two letters of His name, God performs miracles in a hidden manner such as the miracle of Purim. (The miracle of Purim occurred after the destruction of the first Temple.)

The Three Pillars

The *Tur* (written by Rabbeinu Ya'akov ben Asher, a fifteenth-century scholar) (Choshen Mishpat section 1) quotes two Mishnahs from Ethics of the Fathers that seem to contradict each other. The first Mishnah quotes a statement from Shimon the Righteous, who teaches that the world stands on three things: Torah, Temple Service, and Acts of Kindness (1:3). He then quotes another Mishnah from Ethics (1:18) where Rabbi Shimon ben Gamliel teaches that there are three things that sustains the world: judgment, truth, and peace.

This apparent contradiction is resolved by Rabbeinu Yonah (a thirteenth-century scholar). He explains that the first Mishnah is teaching us why the world was created—that being Torah, Temple Service, and

Acts of Kindness. The second Mishnah is explaining why the world remains in existence, and the reasons given are judgment, truth, and peace.

The Bet Yoseph (commentary on the Tur) asks: Why do we need three different reasons to sustain the world? The three reasons given that allowed the world to be created should be reason enough to sustain the world. Why do we need another three things to sustain it?

The Bet Yoseph answers: The two rabbis were addressing two different periods of Jewish history. Shimon the Righteous lived during the period of the first Temple; he therefore could include Temple service in his list. Rabbi Shimon ben Gamliel lived after the destruction of the Temple; he therefore could not include Temple service. Likewise, due to the fact that we are in exile, we cannot properly fulfill the other two pillars: the study of Torah and acts of kindness. He therefore chose three other pillars: judgment, truth, and peace.

The explanation of the Bet Yoseph will enable us to understand a Midrash. The Midrash states that the ministering angels asked God, "On what does the world stand?" God responded as follows:

Let the earth sprout vegetation. (Bereishit 1:11)

This response by God needs to be understood. The Hebrew word used in the Torah for *vegetation* is *desha*—spelled *dalet, shin, aleph.* These three letters spell the three Hebrew world of *din* (judgment), *shalom* (peace), and *emet* (truth). God, in His response, was alluding to the three pillars mentioned by Rabbi Shimon ben Gamliel.[88]

No Animals or Birds

The Prophet Yermiyahu writes:

Both the fowl of the heavens and the beast have fled
and are gone. (Yermiyahu 9:9)

---

88. *Amudei Yehonatan*

The prophet is teaching us that after the destruction of the first Temple, when the Jewish people were banished from the Land of Israel, all the animals and birds also left Israel.

The animals' departure should be viewed as a blessing. If the animals would have remained in Israel, they would have destroyed all the vegetation. Since the animals also left when the Jewish people returned in the times of Ezra, the land was aplenty with vegetation.

This understanding of the verse in Yermiyahu is alluded to in a verse by the Prophet Yeshayahu:

> For a fortified city is solitary, a dwelling is forsaken and abandoned like a pasture; there a calf shall graze, and there he shall lie and consume its branches. (Yeshayahu 27:10)

"For a fortified city" (referring to the city of Jerusalem) is "solitary" even from animals and birds. However, "a dwelling" refers to the mountain of Seir where the descendants of Esau reside, is "forsaken and abandoned"—no humans reside there, like the desert. The verse concludes "Like a pasture there a calf shall graze, and there he shall lie and consume its branches." This means that the animals remained in Seir, and they destroyed all the vegetation, unlike what occurred in the city of Jerusalem.[89]

Many Kings

The Prophet Yermiyahu writes:

> For behold I am summoning all the families of the kingdoms of the north, says the Lord, and they will come and place, each one his throne at the entrance of the gates of Jerusalem. (Yermiyahu 1:15)

This verse should be understood as an act of great mercy by God.

---

89. *Ahavat Yehonatan*

If only one king would have ruled Israel, there would be no other king or nation who could stop that king from destroying the Jewish people. Now that the Jewish people were ruled by many kings, no king could act alone and destroy the Jewish people. There would always be among the many kings some who would not consent to the annihilation of the Jewish people.[90]

Black Shoes

The Talmud (Bava Kamma 59b) records the following event: Eliezer Ze'era once put on a pair of black shoes and stood in the marketplace of Nehardea. When the attendance of the house of the Exilarch met him there, they said to him: "What grounds have you for wearing black shoes?" He said to them, "I am mourning for Jerusalem." They said to him, "Are you such a distinguished person as to mourn over Jerusalem?"

What is the significance of this? When the Temple was in existence, there was an outpouring of God's Holy Spirit and many individuals received God's prophecy, or His Holy Spirit. Wherever God's Holy Spirit was found, one had to remove one's shoes, as is seen when God tells Moshe to remove his shoes before coming close to the burning bush.

However, after the destruction of the Temple, God's presence was removed; therefore, there was no need to remove one's shoes. Wearing black shoes was seen as a symbol of mourning for the destruction of the Temple.

Why did the Exilarch's men question Eliezer and ask him, "Are you worthy of mourning Jerusalem in the manner that you do?"

When the Temple existed, only men of great stature would receive God's Holy Spirit. They therefore asked Eliezer, "If you would have been living in the times of the Temple, would you have been of such greatness to receive God's Holy Spirit? If you answer yes, we can understand that you are mourning by wearing black shoes. If you answer no,

---

90. *Ahavat Yehonatan*

even in the times of the Temple, you would not have to remove your shoes. Now that the Temple is destroyed, you should not express your mourning by wearing black shoes."[91]

The Ultimate Redemption

The Talmud (Sanhedrin 98b) discusses the pains that will engulf the world prior to the coming of Moshiach. They will be so severe that many rabbis stated, "Let him come, but let me not see him."

The reason the period prior to Moshiach's arrival will be so severe is because when the Jewish people went into exile, God went into exile as well. God went into exile to protect the Jewish people.

In the Messianic era, God and the Jewish people will not return to Israel at the same time. God will return to Israel prior to the Jewish people returning to Israel. God needs to be in Israel prior to the ingathering of the Jewish people as many things need to be accomplished before the Jewish people arrive. These things cannot be accomplished unless God has already returned to the Land of Israel.

If this is the case, then the Jewish people will be in the diaspora without God's protection, and as a result, the Jewish people will experience great persecution.[92]

Darkness

Why will the Jewish people experience so much darkness and persecution prior to their redemption? Prior to a new entity coming into existence, there has to be concealment.

By creation, the Torah says, "And the earth was astonishingly empty," and then God said, "Let there be light," and there was light. First concealment ("the earth was astonishingly empty") and then the new entity ("let there be light"). Likewise, a seed planted in the ground first needs to rot before it can grow into a tree.

---

91. *Yaaroth Devash*

92. *Tiferet Yehonatan*

Similarly, prior to the coming of Moshiach, the nations of the world will persecute the Jewish people, and in the midst of the darkness, the Redeemer will come.

The Snake

> Moshe answered and said, "Behold they will not believe, and they will not heed my voice, but they will say, 'The Lord has not appeared to you.'" And the Lord said to him, "What is that in your hand?" And he said, "A staff." And He said, "Cast it to the ground," and he cast it to the ground and it became like a serpent, and Moshe fled from before it. And the Lord said to Moshe, "Stretch forth your hand and take hold of its tail." So Moshe stretched forth his hand and grasped it, and it became a staff in his hand. (Shemot 4:1–4)

This conversation between God and Moshe can be understood in the following manner:

If, on their own, the Jewish people would not awaken to do *teshuvah* (repent), God would subjugate the Jewish people as he did in the times of Haman. The Jewish people will repent and will be worthy of the final redemption. (Talmud Sanhedrin 97b)

The verse can be understood as follows: "Behold they will not believe, and they will not heed my voice," means the Jewish people are not worthy of being redeemed. God tells Moshe to take the staff, and Moshe cast it to the ground, and it became like a serpent. The snake represents Haman. "Moshe fled from before it," means that Moshe was worried that perhaps the Jewish people would not be able to endure the suffering at the hands of Haman. Therefore, God said to Moshe, "Stretch forth your hand and take hold of its tail . . . and it became a staff in your hand." God was impressing upon Moshe that the Jewish people would be able to overcome its enemies.

Based on the above, why have the Jewish people been in exile for such a long duration? God could have subjugated the Jewish people at the hands of a king as evil as Haman. The Jewish people would repent, and we could usher in the Messianic era.

For the Moshiach to come, the Jewish people need to atone for all of the collective sins of the Jewish people throughout the centuries. It isn't sufficient to be persecuted by an evil empire. Even though we have been persecuted, we still need to atone for our sins to herald in the Messianic era.[93]

Yishmael and Esau

> *"I will gather all the nations to Jerusalem to do battle"*
> (Zechariah 14:2)

The Zohar writes that the downfall of the Edomites (descendants of Esau) needs to take place in the Land of Israel since Yitzchak gave Esau and his descendants Mount Seir as an inheritance. Yitzchak also told Esau:

> *You will live by your sword* (Bereishit 27:40)

When Moshe and the Jewish people were traveling in the desert, God said to Moshe:

> *You shall not provoke them (the Edomites) for I will not give you any of their land not so much as a footstep, because I have given Mount Seir to Esau for an inheritance.* (Devarim 2:5)

Moshe approached the Edomites and he requested:

> *Please let us pass through your land; we will not pass through fields or vineyards, nor will we drink well water. We will walk along the king's road, and we will turn neither to the right nor to the left until we have passed through your territory.* (Bamidbar 20:17)

---

93. *Ahavat Yehonatan*

The Edomites responded:

You shall not pass through me, lest I go out towards you with the sword. (Bamidbar 20:19)

The Edomites were living on land promised to them by Yitzchak; therefore, the Jewish people were not permitted to conquer their land. Therefore, the Edomites would be destroyed when they enter the Land of Israel, as the Prophet Ovadiah writes:

And saviors will ascend Mt. Zion to judge the Mountain of Esau, and the Lord shall have the kingdom. (Ovadiah 1:21)

The prophet is saying that in the Messianic era, Esau will go and help Yishmael in their battle against the Jewish people. The descendants of Esau will be defeated in the Land of Israel and then "the Lord shall have the kingdom."

Based on the above, we will be able to understand a cryptic conversation recorded in the Talmud (Bechoros 8b) between Rabbi Yehoshua and the wise men of Athens.

The wise men of Athens asked Rabbi Yehoshua, "How does one cut down a field of swords?" Rabbi Yehoshua responded, "With the horns of a donkey."

When the wise men of Athens asked, "How does one cut down a field of swords?" they were asking, "How will the Jewish people defeat the descendants of Esau?" The land of Edom is often referred to as the *field* of Edom. Edomites were blessed to live by the sword. "The field of the sword" is an allusion to the descendants of Esau.

Rabbi Yehoshua responded, "by the horn of the donkey." The Talmud (Yevamot 62a) compares the descendants of Yishmael to a donkey. Rabbi Yehoshua was saying, at the end of days, the Edomites will be defeated when they come to help the Yishmalites in their battle against the Jewish people in the Land of Israel.[94]

---

94. *Ahavat Yehonatan*

Moshiach's Arrival

THE TALMUD (SANHEDRIN 98A) STATES THAT there seems to be a contradiction in a verse from Yeshayahu. The prophet writes, "In its time (will Moshiach come)," while it is also written. "I (the Lord) will hasten it (the coming of Moshiach)."

The Talmud resolves the contradiction by stating that if the Jewish people are worthy, God would hasten the arrival of Moshiach. If they were not worthy, Moshiach would come at the due time.

The Talmudic discussion concerning the arrival of Moshiach sheds light on a verse in Yeshayahu. The Prophet Yeshayahu writes:

I will rejoice with the Lord; my soul shall exult with my God, for He has attired me with garments of salvation, with a robe of righteousness He has enwrapped. (Yeshayahu 61:10)

"I will rejoice with the Lord" means that when the Jewish people repent, God will hasten Moshiach's arrival. "My soul shall exult with my God" refers to if the Jewish people don't repent and the Moshiach comes at the due time. "For He has attired me with garments of salvation" refers to when the Jewish people repent and God redeems us with mercy we will be clothed with garments of honor. "With a robe of righteousness He has enwrapped" refers to if the Jewish people don't repent, we will only be clothed with a garment of righteousness—meaning that God displays His righteousness by redeeming us at the due time even though we are not worthy.[95]

---

95. *Ahavat Yehonatan*

Long Life

The Talmud (Berachot 8a) states, "When they told Reb Yochanan that there were old men in Bavel (Babylonia), he showed astonishment and asked, 'Why is this so? It is written, that your days may be multiplied, and the days of your children upon the land (of Israel), but not outside the land (of Israel).'"

How is it possible that Jewish people are living long lives even though they are not living in Israel? When they told him that the people of Bavel came early to the shul and left late, he said, "That is what helps them."

What is the connection between a long life and coming early and leaving late from a shul? A person who lives in the diaspora and yearns for the rebuilding of the Temple, God considers it as if that person is living in Israel and can be rewarded with long life. This is true only if the person doesn't act in a manner that would cause a lengthier duration in exile. An example of this is recorded in the same section of the Talmud. The Talmud states that if there is a shul in a city and a person does not attend, the person is punished with exile.

When Reb Yochanon heard, concerning the Jewish people in Bavel, that not only did they come to shul but they came early and left late, then of course they would be blessed with a long life.[96]

The Great Redeemer

We refer to God as a strong redeemer. How are we to understand this description of God?

God relates to the world in two ways. By the laws of nature and, at times, beyond the laws of nature—meaning in a miraculous manner.

When God runs the world based on nature, He is running the world based on strict judgment. The Hebrew word for *the nature* is *HaTeVA hei-tet-beit-ayin*; the numerical value of the word *HaTeVA* is 86. The name of God that represents strict justice is the name *Elokim.*

---

96. *Keshet Yehonatan*

The numerical value of *Elokim* is 86. We now see the link between strict justice and nature.

When God relates to the world beyond the laws of nature, He is relating to the world with *chesed* (kindness). The Midrash tells us that when the Jewish people were by the Reed Sea, God appeared as a mighty warrior. The reason He appeared as such was because the Jewish people were not worthy of being redeemed. God had to act beyond the laws of nature to redeem the Jewish people. He therefore is portrayed as a mighty warrior.

We therefore plead to God and say that even though we are not worthy because of our sins, *You are a redeemer of great strength,* and you can go beyond the laws of nature and redeem us just as you redeemed the Jewish people from Egypt and you split the sea.

The Four Lepers

In Melachim II, it says:

> *There were four men stricken with tzora'as at the entrance of the gate* (Melachim II 7:3)

Tzora'as is a miraculous affliction of the skin that occurred as a punishment for idle talk or gossip. The chapter continues in great detail how these four stricken men informed the Jewish people of how God had performed a great miracle for the Jewish people.

A question can be asked: Why did God choose men who were stricken to be the ones to inform the Jewish people of the great miracle?

The Talmud (Sanhedrin 98a) states that Moshiach will come under two very different circumstances: Either when the whole Jewish world is righteous or when the whole Jewish world are sinners.

We can understand Moshiach coming when the Jewish people are all righteous. How are we to understand the opposite scenario—that God will come when the Jewish people are all sinners?

God had made a promise to Abraham that He would never exchange the Jewish people for another nation.

When the Jewish people were in Egypt, we had reached the forty-ninth level of impurity. If we would have fallen to the fiftieth level, we would have reached a point of impurity that God would have had to destroy the Jewish people—something He could not do because of His promise to Abraham. God therefore had to redeem the Jewish people.

The law of a person afflicted with *tzora'as* is that if a person has a single white hair, he is considered impure. If, however, his whole body turns white, he is considered not afflicted; he is considered pure.

Based on this law, we can now understand why God wanted the Jewish people to discover that they had defeated the enemy by the four men afflicted. Even though the Jewish people may not be worthy, they will be redeemed. Just as a man who is completely white will be considered not afflicted.

We will be able to understand the second question we posed: Why if the Jewish people are all sinners will God redeem them? God will have to redeem them to fulfill His promise to Abraham of never exchanging the Jewish people for another nation.[97]

They Did Not Forsake God

The Lord will judge the ends of the earth. And He will give great
strength to His King. And raise the horn of His anointed one.
(Shmuel I 2:10)

This verse can be understood to be referring to the Messianic period.

"The Lord will judge the ends of the earth" is referring to the idol worshippers, whom God will judge at the end of days.

"And He will give great strength to His King" refers to King David.

"And raise the horn of His anointed one" means that the Jewish people will be victorious in judgment, and they will merit the arrival of Moshiach. And Moshiach will be elevated and exalted among the nations. The nations will say that the Jewish people suffered so greatly

---

97. *Ahavat Yehonatan*

in exile, and they did not forsake their God. Therefore, they will leave the exile with great joy speedily in our day.[98]

Why Wednesday?

The Midrash states that every Wednesday, the children of Korach utter the cry, "When will we be removed from the large hole in the ground?!" The children of Korach had been swallowed alive by the ground when they rebelled against Moshe.

Why did they cry out specifically on Wednesday? The rabbis teach us that the final redemption will be similar to the redemption from Egypt. The Jewish people left Egypt on a Thursday. Likewise, the final redemption will take place on a Thursday. In Malachi 3:23, the prophet writes:

> Behold I will send you Elijah the Prophet before the coming of
> the great and awesome day of the Lord.

If Moshiach will redeem the Jewish people on Thursday similar to when the Jewish people left Egypt, Elijah will arrive the day before, on a Wednesday. Therefore, every Wednesday the children of Korach cry out to Elijah that he should save them.

The Jewish People of Spain

> Why have I come and there is no man? Why have I called and
> no one answers? (Yeshayahu 50:2)

What is the prophet referring to? The rabbis teach us that if the Jewish people would have returned with Ezra the Scribe *en masse* to rebuild the second Temple, we would have merited the final redemption.

The fifteenth-century scholar Abarbanel writes that the Jewish people's suffering during the time of the Spanish Inquisition was a

---

98. *Ahavat Yehonatan*

result of the Jewish people living in Spain who did not return with Ezra the Scribe to rebuild the second Temple.

We will now understand the above words of the prophet. God is calling out to the Jewish people in the diaspora to return with Ezra the Scribe; however, no one wanted to go.

Yeshayahu's Vision

The vision of Isaiah the son of Amoz, which he saw concerning Judah and Jerusalem, in the days of Uzziah, Jotham, Ahaz, and Hezekiah, kings of Judah. (Yeshayahu 1:1)

The Prophet Yeshayahu prophesized during the era of four kings: Uzziah, Jotham, Ahaz, and Hezekiah. Uzziah and Ahaz were wicked, while Jotham and Hezekiah were righteous.

The Hebrew word used for *vision* in our verse is *chazon*; the word *chazon* is spelled *chet-zayin-vov-nun*. These four letters are an acronym for *chatzyeho zoam vchatzyeho nechamah*—meaning that half (of the kings of Yeshayahu's era) were evil, while half (of the kings) were righteous.[99]

The Secret

Why didn't God reveal to the prophets when the final redemption will occur?

The Talmud (Sanhedrin 97b) says Moshiach can come at any time, as the verse in Tehillim (Psalms) 95:7 states that (Moshiach) can come *today* if you will listen to his voice.

If God would reveal to the prophets the day of Moshiach's arrival, Moshiach would not be able to come prior to that date even if the Jewish people had repented and were worthy of being redeemed.[100]

Another reason given for why God concealed the time of the

---

99. *Ahavat Yehonatan*

100. *Ahavat Yehonatan*

ultimate redemption is that if the Jewish people were told when Moshiach would arrive, they would not have been able to bear the pain and suffering of our lengthy exile. Being we don't know the date, each time we experience great suffering, we can attribute it to the birth pains of Moshiach, and we do not lose hope.

We see this by Rabbi Akiva who lived a short time after the destruction of the second Temple, and he believed that Bar Kokhba was the Moshiach.[101]

A further reason offered is: One of the fundamentals of Jewish faith is free choice. As the Talmud states, when a child is born, heaven does not declare if this person will grow to be a *tzaddik* (righteous person) or a *rasha* (evil person).

If the date of the Messianic arrival would have been proclaimed, all the people living till that time could not have been all righteous, because if they were, Moshiach should have come earlier. In a sense then, the free choice of being righteous would have been taken from them. Therefore, God did not reveal the date of the coming of Moshiach.[102]

Persecution

During our lengthy exile, we have endured an endless amount of persecution at the hands of the Edomites (the descendants of Esau).

The Arizal writes that the pogroms that spread through Germany and Spain were all auspicious moments for the final redemption. However, the Jewish people did not do *teshuva* (repent) and the attribute of strict justice prevailed, and this resulted in great destruction in the world.[103]

Day Break

The darkest part of the night is just before sunrise. So it will be at the

---

101. *Yaaroth Devash*

102. *Yaaroth Devash*

103. *Ahavat Yehonatan*

time of the final redemption. The Jewish people will experience terrible suffering; the Jewish people will experience God's attribute of strict justice. And, in the midst of their suffering, the Jewish people will be redeemed. This is alluded to in Shmuel II 22:13:

From the brightness before Him flamed forth coals of fire.

The Hebrew word used in the verse for brightness is *nogah*, which also means the morning star. The verse can be understood to mean, "From the brightness before Him" (prior to day break) "flamed forth coals of fire," symbolizing God's attribute of strict justice.[104]

The Sun Shone Brightly

The Zohar writes that the night the Jewish people left Egypt the sun shone bright throughout the night. Why did this occur?

The Torah states:

And it was at midnight and the Lord smote every firstborn.
(Shemot 12:29)

Until midnight, God was judging the Jewish people to see whether they merited to be redeemed from Egypt. At midnight, they passed judgment and were redeemed from Egypt.

The Midrash (Bereishit Rabbah 50:3) states that the Jewish people can only be judged during the day. Therefore, the night of the exodus, God performed a miracle, and the sun shone bright that night in order to judge the Jewish people.

We can now understand the words of Zechariah the Prophet:

And it shall be one day that shall be known to the Lord, neither day nor night; and it shall come to pass that at evening it shall be light. (Zechariah 14:7)

---

104. *Ahavat Yehonatan*

Prior to the coming of Moshiach, the Jewish people will be judged. This judgement can only take place during the day. Zechariah therefore prophesized on that day of judgment "at evening it shall be light" to enable the judgment to take place.[105]

Returning to Israel

At the time of the ultimate redemption, there will be terrible decrees against the Jewish people living in the diaspora. Many Jewish people will go and live in the Land of Israel. God will hear their crying and will send Moshiach.[106]

Assyria and Egypt

> *And it shall come to pass on that day, that a great shofar shall be sounded, and those lost in the land of Assyria and those exiled in the land of Egypt shall come and they shall prostrate themselves before the Lord on the holy mount in Jerusalem.*
> (Yeshayahu 27:13)

Many ask the question: What will happen to the Jewish people who don't live in Assyria and Egypt?

The Jewish people who Sancheriv sent into exile will be gathered together in the land of Assyria. The Jewish people who went into exile after the destruction of the second Temple will gather together in the land of Egypt. From there, they will return to Jerusalem.

We now can understand a verse in Yechezkel. The verse reads:

> *And say to them, so says the Lord God: Behold I will take the children of Israel from among the nations where they have gone, and I will gather them from every side, and I will bring them to their land.* (Yechezkel 37:21)

---

105. *Ahavat Yehonatan*

106. *Ahavat Yehonatan*

When the verse says, "and I will gather them from every side," this refers to the Jewish people who have gathered in the land of Egypt that borders the Land of Israel. After they have been gathered in Egypt, God says, "and I will bring them to their land," meaning the Land of Israel.

Equal Footing

And saviors will ascend Mount Zion to judge the Mountain of Esau, and the kingdom will be God's (Ovadia 1:21)

This verse demonstrates the righteousness of the Jewish people. The Jewish people have the full right to seek retribution against the descendants of Esau for the pain and suffering they inflicted on the Jewish people through the course of their history. However, they will not seek God's retribution because of their suffering. They will seek it because it is the will of God.

When Rivkah, the wife of Yitzchak, was pregnant carrying Ya'akov and Esau, God appeared to her and said:

Two nations are in your womb, and two kingdoms will separate from your innards, and one kingdom will become mightier than the other (Bereishit 25:23)

Rashi explains that the two nations—the descendants of Ya'akov and the descendants of Esau—can never be of equal greatness, when one rises the other must fall.

The verse quoted above explains why the Jewish people seek the downfall of Esau's descendants. The phrase "And saviors will ascend Mount Zion" refers to the coming of Moshiach, and at the end of the verse, "and the kingdom will be God's" refers to the rebuilding of the Temple. If so, the descendants of Esau cannot be on equal footing; they will need to be punished to fulfill the word of God to Rivkah many millennia prior.

The Astronomers

The Prophet Yeshayahu writes:

> *The voice of your watchmen they raise their voice, they sing*
> *glad songs in unison, with their own eyes they will see that*
> *God returns to Zion.* (Yeshayahu 52:8)

This verse can be understood to mean that prior to the arrival of Moshiach, the astronomers will notice a change in the formation of the stars ("the watchmen . . . with their own eyes they will see"). They will reach the conclusion that this is due to the arrival of Moshiach. "They raise their voice" means that they will inform the Jewish people that Moshiach is coming.

Sound of the Shofar

> *And it shall come to pass on that day, that a great shofar*
> *shall be sounded, and those lost in the land of Assyria.*
> (Yeshayahu 27:13)

When the prophet says, "a great shofar shall be sounded," it doesn't necessarily mean there will be an incredible loud sound coming from a shofar. Rather, God will perform such incredible miracles that it will awaken the whole world and herald in the Messianic era as if it were the piercing sound of the shofar.

When the prophet says it will be the sound of the shofar, the prophet is alluding to the following: The shape of the shofar is straight and then bends at the end; this is similar to the shape of the letter *vov*, which is straight and bends at the end.

The letter *vov* can be spelled *vov-vov*, giving us the numerical value of 12, corresponding to the 12 tribes. The letter *vov* can also be spelled *vov-aleph-vov*, giving us the numerical value of 13. This corresponds to the 13 *shofarot* that were used in the Temple. The third way of writing *vov* is *vov-yud-vov*, which gives us the numerical value of 22. Twenty-two corresponds to the 22 letters of the Hebrew Aleph-Bet.[107]

Accepted by All

When Moshe was informed by God that he would not lead the Jewish people into the Land of Israel, Moshe requested, *'Let the Lord, the God of spirits of all flesh, appoint a man over the congregation, who will go forth before them and come before them, who will lead them out and bring them in, so that the congregation of the Lord will not be like sheep without a shepherd.'* God should appoint a leader who will be accepted by all.

Likewise, the Prophet Yechezkel writes:

> *One king shall be to them all as a king.* (Yechezkel 37:22)

The prophet is impressing upon us that Moshiach will be a leader who will be accepted by all.[108]

Completely Righteous

> *And a shoot shall spring forth from the stem of Yishai,*
> *and a twig shall sprout from his roots.* (Yeshayahu 11:1)

Yishai was the father of King David. (Moshiach will be a descendant of King David.) The Talmud (Shabbat 55b) states that Yishai's righteousness was such that he did not pass away because of any sin that he had committed as he was sinless. The reason he passed away was because God had decreed, no man shall live forever as a punishment for Adam and Chava eating from the tree of knowledge. Likewise, Yishai's descendant Moshiach will be completely righteous without sin.[109]

---

107. *Ahavat Yehonatan*

108. *Ahavat Yehonatan*

109. *Ahavat Yehonatan*

At the Gates of Rome

The Torah begins with the verse:

In the beginning of God's creation of the heavens and the earth. Now the earth was astonishingly empty and darkness was on the face of the deep and the spirit of God was hovering over the face of the water. (Bereishit 1:1–2)

The Zohar explains that "Now the earth was astonishingly empty" refers to the idol worshippers who will inhabit the world. God wanted to destroy the world at that point. The reason He didn't was because God saw the ultimate arrival of Moshiach. This is alluded to in the next verse, as it says:

And God said, "Let there be light" and there was light.

The light is referring to the light of Moshiach. This understanding of the opening verses of the Torah will help us comprehend a statement recorded in the Talmud (Sanhedrin 98a). The Talmud states that Moshiach is sitting at the gates of Rome.

This is not meant to be taken literally; rather, the world should have been destroyed because the Roman Empire were idol worshippers. The world was not destroyed because "Moshiach is sitting at the gates of Rome." Moshiach will bring light to the world, and the light will be the counterbalance to the darkness of the idol worshippers.[110]

The Temple in Heaven

Widen the place of your tent, and let them stretch forth the curtains of your habitations, do not spare; lengthen your cords and strengthen your stakes. For right and left shall you prevail, and your seed shall inherit nations and repopulate desolate cities. (Yeshayahu 54:2–3)

---

110. *Ahavat Yehonatan*

The verse in Yeshayahu can be understood as follows: The Prophet Yechezkel (Yechezkel 43) writes that God will make the third Temple larger than the previous Temples. The rabbis teach us that directly opposite the physical Temple in Jerusalem in heaven is a spiritual replica of the Temple below. When the prophet writes, "Widen the place of your tent," he is referring to the third Temple, which will be larger than the previous Temples.

If the Temple below will be larger, then the Temple in heaven will be larger as well. King David in Tehillim (Psalms) 104:2 writes:

Spread your heavens like a curtain.

The heavens are compared to a curtain. When the prophet says, "let them stretch forth the curtains of your habitations," he is referring to the Temple in heaven, which will become larger since the Temple on earth has become larger.[111]

The Largest Temple

Why will the third Temple be larger than the previous two? The Temple was built in Jerusalem at the epicenter of the Land of Israel. When Moshiach will come, the Jewish people will inherit the lands of Kini, Kenezi, and Kadmoni. They will also inherit the lands of Sodom and Gomorrah. The Temple will have to be larger in order for it to remain the epicenter of the Land of Israel.

This is alluded to in the words of the Prophet Yeshayahu:

For right and left shall you prevail, and your seed shall inherit nations and repopulate desolate cities. (Yeshayahu 54:3)

"For right and left shall you prevail" refers to the lands of Kini, Kenezi, and Kadmoni, "and your seed shall inherit nations and repopulate desolate cities" refers to the barren cities of Sodom and Gomorrah.[112]

---

111. *Ahavat Yehonatan*

112. *Ahavat Yehonatan*

Birth of Moshiach

The Jerusalem Talmud (Berachot 2:4) states that on the very same day the Temple was destroyed, Moshiach—the ultimate redeemer of the Jewish people—was born.

The Talmud (Yoma 54b) states that when the enemy entered the holy of holies, they saw the ark, and the two cherubim that were placed on top of the ark were facing one another.

The Talmud (Bava Batra 99a) quotes two verses that seem to be contradicting each other. In Shemot 25:20), the verse implies that the cherubim were facing each other. However, in Divrei Hayamim 3:13), the verse tells us that the cherubim were not facing each other; rather, they were each facing the exterior walls, meaning they had their backs to each other.

The Talmud in Bava Batra resolves the contradiction in the following manner: The two cherubim represented God and the Jewish people. When the Jewish people were following and fulfilling God's commands, the cherubim would face each other, indicating the love between God and the Jewish people. However, when the Jewish people were not fulfilling God's commands, the cherubim would turn their backs on each other.

The fourteenth-century scholar Ritva poses the following question based on the Talmudic sources quoted above. How can we say that when the enemy entered the holy of holies, they saw the cherubim facing each other? The cherubim facing each other indicates the great love between God and the Jewish people. How can we speak of such great love on the very day the Temple was destroyed?

The two cherubim were facing each other, indicating the love between God and His people, since on the day the Temple was destroyed, God forgave the Jewish people, and this is apparent since on that very day Moshiach was born.[113]

---

113. *Ahavat Yehonatan*

The Messianic Era

What Will Happen?

There is an argument recorded in the Talmud (Sanhedrin 99a) concerning what will occur when Moshiach comes. One opinion is that all the prophecies of miraculous occurrences will occur. God will remove all impurities from the world. The world will become a totally new world.

The second opinion is the opinion of Shmuel, who states the world as we know it will not change with one exception: The Jewish people will no longer be subservient to other nations. The Jewish people will be free to serve God.

In truth, there is no disagreement between the two opinions. Initially with the arrival of Moshiach, we will experience freedom, and we will be able to serve God without the fear of persecution. During this period of time, if the Jewish people will fully embrace God and fulfill all His commandments, we will merit all the miracles and wonders recorded in the Books of the Prophets.[114]

The Spiritual Level of Abraham

At the time of the Messianic era, the Jewish people will be on the spiritual level of Abraham. This idea is seen in the following verses. Concerning Abraham it is written:

He made his sword like dust. (Yeshayahu 41:2)

---

114. *Yaaroth Devash*

The Talmud (Taanit 21a) explains this verse to mean that wherever Abraham went and confronted his enemies, the dust would turn into swords and protect him.

During the Messianic era, the Jewish people will also be protected in a similar fashion. This is alluded to by the Prophet Yeshayahu when he writes:

And they shall lick the dust of your feet. (Yeshayahu 49:23)

This is referring to the Messianic era when the enemies of the Jewish people will see how the dust is protecting the Jewish people.

To Pray

The Talmud in (Berachot 32a) states that when a person begins to pray, he should begin by praising God and then pray for their needs. Throughout our lengthy exile, one of the challenges we have faced is to have the composure and frame of mind to be able to pray with complete sincerity and devotion.

However, when Moshiach comes, we will no longer be in servitude and we will have peace of mind to pray as we should. This is alluded to by the Prophet Yeshayahu:

And you shall say on that day, "Thank the Lord call in His Name, publicize His deeds among the peoples."
(Yeshayahu 12:4)

The verse can be understood as follows: "And you shall say on that day," refers to the day of Moshiach's arrival. "Thank the Lord" is to begin our davening by offering praise to God. "Call in His Name," is to begin to ask our requests from God. "Publicize His deeds among the peoples" is to inform the world of the great kindness bestowed upon us by God after we have concluded davening.[115]

---

115. *Ahavat Yehonatan*

Vision

Because of their holiness, certain foods could only be eaten in Jerusalem. The Talmud (Megillah 9b) states that one doesn't have to be physically in Jerusalem to eat these foods. Even if one had left the walls of Jerusalem, as long as one could still see Jerusalem, he could eat the consecrated food.

The Talmud says that one could still see Jerusalem from a village called Tzofim. (The word *tzofim* means *to see*.)

The Arizal writes that the word *tzofeh* (from the same root word as *tzofim*) means *prophecy*. As long as one can see Jerusalem, one can draw from and comprehend *Ruach HaKodesh* (the Divine Spirit). However, once a person had passed Tzofim and could no longer see Jerusalem, one couldn't connect with the Divine Spirit.

A person can see great distances over flat land. If, however, there are hills and mountains that is blocking his vision, the length he can see will be dependent on how close or far the mountains are. We can now appreciate the words of the Prophet Zechariah as he discusses the Messianic era:

> *The whole earth shall be changed to be like a plain, from the hill of Rimmon in the south of Jerusalem; but it (Jerusalem) will be elevated high and remain in its old place. (Zechariah 14:10)*

In the times of Moshiach, the Jewish people will be beloved by God, and they will bask in God's glory. There won't be any mountains, so to speak, that will infringe on the Jewish people's ability to see God's glory.

Completely Pure

Note: The laws of purity and impurity apply to what a person consumes. If a person who is in a state of impurity touches food, he will cause the food to be considered impure as well. If a second person will eat from the impure food, that person will also be considered impure.

The Talmud (Hagigah 26a) writes one shouldn't accept food from an ignorant individual since we suspect the person to be in a state of impurity and had transmitted the impurity to the food. However, on a festival, we do not suspect the ignorant person to be impure, and we would be permitted to eat his food. The reason why on a festival the law is different is because, prior to the festival, everyone, including the ignorant, are obligated to immerse themselves in a *mikvah* (ritual bath), thereby purifying themselves, and they will not be transferring impurity to the foods they will touch.

The *Nasi* (Prince) of the Jewish people is considered to be in a state of purity all year long.

We will now appreciate the prophecy of Yechezkel on a deeper level.

I will sprinkle clean water upon you and you will be clean.
(Yechezkel 36:25)

In the Messianic era, everyone (including the ignorant) will be in a state of purity.

The Prophet Yechezkel also prophesized:

It shall be incumbent on all of the people of the land to give this gift to the prince of Israel. (Yechezkel 45:16)

The verse can be translated to mean that "It shall be incumbent on all of the people of the land to give this gift." All of the Jewish people, including the ignorant, will be fit to consume *Terumah* (consecrated food) since they are all in a state of purity (as seen in the earlier quoted verse).

The last phrase of the verse—"to the prince of Israel"—means that just as the prince of Israel is considered pure and the food he touches pure the whole year round, so too will the ignorant people have that same status in the times of Moshiach.[116]

---

116. *Ahavat Yehonatan*

No Jew Will Be Left Behind

At the time of the ultimate redemption, all Jewish people will be part of the ingathering and return to the Land of Israel—even those Jewish people who do not know that they are Jewish will return. How will those individuals who have no idea they are Jewish become aware that they are indeed part of the Jewish people?

Prior to the Jewish people leaving Egypt, God brought the ten plagues upon the Egyptians. Similarly, at the time of the final redemption, God will bring ten plagues upon the world. Those individuals who are part of the Jewish people but do not know so will be spared together with the rest of the Jewish people. By being spared, they will come to the recognition that they are also part of the Jewish people.

This idea is alluded to in the prophecy of Yeshayahu. The prophet writes:

> I will place a sign upon them, and I will send from them refugees to the nations. (Yeshayahu 66:19)

The verse can be understood in the following manner: "Them" is referring to the individuals who do not know that they are Jewish. "I will place a sign" means "I will perform miracles that will distinguish between the Jewish people and the rest of humanity." And "I will send from them refugees," means that those individuals who will be spared will join and become part of the Jewish people.

The Lost Jewish People of Spain and Portugal

The Abarbanel explains that in the Messianic era, the Jewish people of Spain and Portugal who were forced to abandon their faith at the time of the Inquisition will return. And not only will they become part of the Jewish people, but they will also be elevated and will become part of the priests and the Levites. This is alluded to by the Prophet Yeshayahu when he writes:

From them too will I take for priests and for Levites.
(Yeshayahu 66:21)

The words *"them too"* is referring to the Jewish people of Spain and Portugal who were forced to convert. Even though these Jewish people have fully assimilated among the gentiles, God will awaken within them a desire to reconnect with the Jewish people.

This is alluded to in the verse:

The remnant of Jacob shall be in the midst of many peoples, like dew sent by the Lord. (Micha 5:6)

"The remnant of Jacob shall be in the midst of many peoples" refers to the assimilated Jewish people of Spain and Portugal. "Like dew sent by the Lord" means, unlike rain where at times we need to pray for rain, dew is always found on the ground without any prayers from man. Likewise, those assimilated Jewish people who don't even know they are Jewish will return without any input of their own.

The Righteous and the Wicked

The Talmud (Shabbat 30b) states that in the Messianic era, the nature of the world will change. A woman will give birth every day. They also will not have birth pangs. How are we then to understand the prophecy of Yeshayahu, who says:

And kings shall be your nursing fathers and their princesses your wet nurses. (Yeshayahu 49:23)

According to the Talmud, in the times of Moshiach, will there be no need for wet nurses? To resolve this question, we need to introduce the opinion of Shmuel quoted in the Talmud. Shmuel writes that in the Messianic era, the world will be the same as we know it. The difference will be that there will be world peace, and the Jewish people will not be subjugated, and they will be free to serve God.

How is Shmuel's opinion consistent with all the prophecies recorded in the Books of Prophets that speak of Moshiach's arrival ushering in a world full of miracles?

The righteous will merit all the miracles recorded in the Books of Prophets and in the Talmud, while in Shmuel's opinion, for the wicked, the experience will be that the world remains the same. When the Prophet Yeshayahu writes, "their princesses your wet nurses," this is what the wicked will experience. When the Talmud says the women will give birth every day, it is referring to what the righteous will experience.[117]

Young Girls

In the Messianic era, the Land of Israel will be extremely holy. Therefore, only those women who are eligible to marry a Cohen will be able to live in Israel.

The Talmud (Ketubot 11a) writes that a Jewish girl over the age of three who was kidnapped could not marry a Cohen. If she was under the age of three when she was rescued from her kidnappers, she could marry a Cohen. This is alluded to by the Prophet Yeshayahu:

They shall bring your sons in their armpits, and your daughters shall be borne on their shoulders. (Yeshayahu 49:22)

The prophet is referring to the time when the Jewish people will be ingathered to the Land of Israel at the time of their redemption.

Why does the prophet say, "your daughters shall be borne on their shoulders"? The verse is referring to a very young girl who could be carried on one's shoulders; only very young girls who were held in captivity would be permitted to live in Israel.

---

117. *Ahavat Yehonatan*

From the North and South Poles

The Talmud (Shabbat 75a) states that it is a mitzvah to know how to calculate the cycles and the planetary courses. Why is there an obligation to be knowledgeable in the workings of the solar system?

If a person is familiar with the workings of the solar system, one would realize that the sun, the moon, and the planets move along a specific path. For example, the sun's rotation is completed every twenty-eight years. Idol worshippers who worshipped the planets would realize their error if they knew that the planets were fixed to a specific path. Because if they were truly divine, they would not be limited to a specific path of travel.

Likewise, if one is living on the north or south pole, the sun's appearance is limited to a few short months each year. If the sun is indeed a god, it should be visible on the north and south pole as it is visible at the equator. Based on this, we will be able to understand the prophecy of Yermiyahu:

> *To You nations will come from the ends of the earth and say, "Only lies have our fathers handed down to us, emptiness in which there is nothing of any avail." (Yermiyahu 16:19)*

"To You nations will come from the ends of the earth" refers to the gentiles who live in proximity to the north and south pole. "Only lies have our fathers handed down to us" means we are not true idol worshippers; we are simply following in the footsteps of our ancestors, who taught us falsehoods. We really want to serve the true God.

Strict Justice for Whom?

Note: The various names of God mentioned in the scriptures and in our prayers represent a specific character trait that God is expressing at that moment. For example, the name Yud-Hei-Vov-Hei pronounced Adonai represents God of compassion. The name Elokim speaks of the attribute of strict justice.

In the Messianic era, God will be completely compassionate toward the Jewish people. If a Jew will transgress accidentally one of God's commandments, God will need to express His attribute of justice. However, unlike in the pre-Messianic era where God would have punished the Jew for his transgression, in the Messianic era, God will express His attribute of justice and punish the wicked of the nations rather than punish the Jew. This is alluded to in the verse:

So said your Master, the Lord and your God who shall judge
His people (Yeshayahu 51:22)

"So said your Master, the Lord" (*Yud-Hei-Vov-Hei,* pronounced *Adonai*) refers to God of benevolence and kindness, and God will act with the Jewish people with kindness and compassion. "Your God (*Elokim* speaks of the attribute of strict justice) who shall judge His people," refers to God of strict justice, and God will judge the nations of the world with strict justice.

Day or Night

Mankind is able to distinguish between night and day. When the sun shines, we know it is day, and at sunset, we know it is night. Angels in heaven are able to distinguish between day and night, as angels only sing songs of praise to God by day and not by night.

The Talmud (Megillah 10b) states that when the Egyptians were chasing the Jewish people through the Reed Sea, the angels wanted to sing songs of praise to God. God silenced them and told them, "My handiwork are drowning in the sea and you want to sing songs of praise."

At the time of the ultimate redemption, God will seek retribution against those nations who wanted to conquer Jerusalem. The angels at that time will not sing songs of praise to God just as they did not sing songs of praise to God when the Egyptians were drowning in the sea.

We will now understand the prophecy of Zechariah:

*And it shall be one day that shall be known to the Lord, neither
day nor night.* (Zechariah 14:7)

"And it shall be one day" refers to the time of the ultimate redemption when God will seek to punish the nations that attacked Jerusalem. "Neither day nor night"—the angels will not sing praises to God because God's handiwork are dying; therefore, the angels will not be able to know if it is day or night.[118]

Tithe

Note: A farmer living in Israel had to give a certain amount of produce per year as tithe. He gave to the poor known as **maaser oni,** *to the Levite known as* **maaser rishon** *(the first tithe), and a certain amount of produce had to be taken and eaten by its owner in Jerusalem known as* **maaser sheni** *(the second tithe.)*

In the Messianic era, there will no longer be an obligation to give tithe to the poor as there no longer will be poor people among the Jewish nation.

There will also no longer be an obligation to give tithe to the Levite. Tithe was given to the Levite since the tribe of the Levites did not receive a portion in the Land of Israel. They were sustained by the gifts they received from the other tribes. The Talmud (Bava Batra 122a) states that in the Messianic era, the tribe of Levi will receive a portion in the Land of Israel. They therefore will not need to receive gifts from the other tribes.

The only tithe the Jewish people will be obligated in is *maaser sheni,* produce brought and eaten by its owners in Jerusalem. This is alluded to in the words of the Prophet Yeshayahu:

*But its gatherers shall eat it and they shall praise the Lord, and
its gatherers shall drink it in My holy courts.* (Yeshayahu 62:9)

---

118. *Ahavat Yehonatan*

This verse is referring to the Messianic era. The prophet is saying the only tithe you will be obligated to bring is the one the person himself gathers and will eat in Jerusalem "in My holy courts."[119]

Strict Justice

God initially wanted to create the world based on the attribute of strict justice. God, however, saw that the world could not exist in that manner. He therefore created the world through two attributes: the attributes of justice and kindness. However, in the Messianic era, there will be no evil in the world, and as a result, God will sustain the world based on the attribute of justice.[120]

New Year

The Talmud (Rosh Hashanah 8a) records an argument concerning when the world was created. One opinion says that the world was created on the first day of Tishrei, while the other opinion says that the world was created on the first day of Nisan.

One may suggest that, in truth, there is no disagreement between the two opinions. The opinion who says Rosh Hashanah is on the first of Tishrei is referring to the world as we know it. While the opinion who says Rosh Hashanah is on the first of Nisan is referring to the Messianic era. When Moshiach comes, the New Year will be marked from the first day of Nisan. This understanding is alluded to by the Prophet Yechezkel:[121]

> On the first day of the first month (the first of Nisan) you shall take a young bull without blemish. (Yechezkel 45:18)

This refers to the sacrifice that is brought on Rosh Hashanah.

---

119. *Ahavat Yehonatan*

120. *Ahavat Yehonatan*

121. *Ahavat Yehonatan*

Yom Kippur

The seven days prior to Yom Kippur, the Cohen Gadol (the High Priest) was separated from his family and the Jewish people in preparation for Yom Kippur.

In the Messianic era, Rosh Hashanah will be on the first day of Nisan. Yom Kippur will then be on the tenth day of Nisan. The Cohen Gadol will need to be separated for seven days leading up to the tenth of Nisan. This is alluded to by the Prophet Yechezkel:

> *And so shall you do on seven days in the month, because of mistaken and single minded men.* (Yechezkel 45:20)

This verse refers to the month of Nisan and the phrase "because of mistaken and single minded men" refers to the Cohen Gadol, who may mistakenly become impure. He therefore will need to be separated in preparation for Yom Kippur.

New Torah

> *And you will return and listen to the voice of the Lord, and fulfill all His commandments, which I command you this day.*
> (Devarim 30:8)

The Torah is impressing upon us that the commandments are eternal. Even in the Messianic era, we will be obligated to fulfill all the commandments. How do we reconcile this verse with the following verse:

> *The Torah will go forth from Me (God).* (Yeshayahu 51:4)

The Midrash explains the verse to mean, "A new Torah will go forth from Me," implying that in the Messianic era, there will be a new Torah.

The verse in Devarim is referring to the commandments, meaning the commandments are eternal and they will never change. The verse in Yeshayahu and its rabbinic interpretation are referring to a deeper understanding of the Biblical texts—meaning that when Moshiach comes, the Jewish people will study the Torah at a level they were unable to while in exile. However, the Jewish people will continue to fulfill all the commandments.[122]

Sprinkling and Eating

When an Israelite brought a sacrifice to the Temple, the Cohen would sprinkle the blood on the altar. Once the blood had been sprinkled, the Israelite's sin was atoned for. Likewise, when the Cohen ate from the sacrifice, the Israelite's sin was atoned for.

When eating from the sacrifice, the Cohen would derive personal pleasure, unlike when he would sprinkle the blood where there was no personal pleasure involved. During the Messianic era, the Cohen will be on a spiritual level where he will not derive any pleasure from eating from the sacrifice and the level of atonement will be on par as when the Cohen sprinkles the blood on the altar. This is alluded to by the Prophet Zechariah when he writes:

And the pots in the House of the Lord will be like the sprinkling bowls before the altar (Zechariah 14:20)

"And the pots in the House of the Lord" refers to the Cohen eating from the sacrifice. "Will be like the sprinkling bowls before the altar" implies that eating from the sacrifice will be like sprinkling the blood on the altar.[123]

Meat

The Talmud (Chullin 16b) states that when the Jewish people were in the desert, they ate only the meat of an animal from which part of its flesh had been offered as a sacrifice on the altar. They had no desire to

---

122. *Tiferet Yehonatan*

123. *Ahavat Yehonatan*

eat non-consecrated meat since the eating of the manna removed their desire for food. However, when the Jewish people entered Israel, they ate the flesh of animals even if none of the meat had been offered as a sacrifice, as the verse says:

> You will say, "I will eat meat," because your soul desires
> to eat meat. (Devarim 12:20)

However, in the Messianic era, the Jewish people will be on a higher spiritual level, and they will no longer have a desire to eat non-consecrated meat. This is alluded to by the Prophet Zechariah:

> Every pot in Jerusalem and in Judah will be holy to the
> Lord of Hosts. (Zechariah 14:21)

This means that all the pots of meat will only contain consecrated meat.[124]

Head of the Sanhedrin

Note: Every Hebrew letter has a numerical value. For example, the first letter aleph has a numerical value of one. The letter yud, which is the tenth letter, has a numerical value of ten. The letter chaf, the eleventh letter, has a numerical value of twenty. Another way to attribute a numerical value to a letter is to remove the zero at the end of a number. Thereby, the letter chaf, which generally has a numerical value of twenty, will have the numerical value of two.

When Ya'akov and his family descended to live in Egypt, the Torah states that seventy people descended. The Torah lists the names of each person who went. If you count the names, you only have sixty-nine names. How do we explain the fact that the Torah said *seventy* people descended to Egypt?

The Ibn Ezra answers: Ya'akov was included in the seventy even

---

124. *Ahavat Yehonatan*

though his name was not listed among those that went down to Egypt. The Sanhedrin (the high court) was comprised of seventy rabbis. The head of the Sanhedrin was included in the seventy. Based on the above, we now will be able to understand King David's verse in Tehillim (Psalms) 122:4:5:

> There ascended the tribes, the tribes of God, testimony to Israel,
> to give thanks to the name of the Lord. For there were set thrones
> for judgment, thrones for the house of David.

The verse can be understood to be referring to Ya'akov and his family's descent to Egypt. The word *God* in this verse is spelled *Yud-hei*, which has a numerical value of fifteen. (*Yud* is ten and *hei* is five.)

Sixty-nine people besides Ya'akov went down to Egypt. If you wanted to write the number sixty-nine, you would write the letters *samech-tet*. You can remove the zero from a number, and then the number would be represented by a different Hebrew letter. Removing the zero from sixty leaves you with the number six. The Hebrew letter corresponding to six is *vov*. You now have a *vov* and *tet*. The *vov's* value is six and the *tet's* value is nine. Six plus nine equals fifteen. We see there is a connection between the number sixty-nine that represents the Sanhedrin and the number fifteen, which is the numerical value of one of God's names. We can now understand the verse from Tehillim (Psalms) 122:4:5.

"The tribes of God" refers to sixty-nine individuals. "Testimony to Israel" means these sixty-nine individuals are the members of the Sanhedrin. An additional member was added to the Sanhedrin. He was the head of the Sanhedrin, bringing the Sanhedrin to seventy members.

The head of the Sanhedrin was always a descendant of the house of King David as the verse continues and says, "For there were set thrones for judgment, thrones for the house of David."

We will now be able to understand a verse in Yechezkel that states:

> My servant (King) David shall be their prince forever.
> (Yechezkel 37:25)

"Prince forever" means a descendent from the house of King David will always be the head of the Sanhedrin.[125]

Heart of Stone, Heart of Flesh

The Prophet Yechezkel writes:

> I will remove your heart of stone out of your flesh and I will replace it with a heart of flesh. (Yechezkel 36:26)

The removal of the heart of stone and replacing it with the heart of flesh means God will replace the heart that has been driving us to sin and replace it with a heart that will not desire to sin.

The question is asked: In the Messianic era, if God will remove the evil inclination, and there will be no more impurity or evil in the world, and there will be no desire to sin, why then does God need to give us a new heart to ensure that the Jewish people will not sin?

In the Messianic era, there will no longer be a desire for physical pleasures. The Jewish people will no longer sin for physical desires. However, the Jewish people will sin in a manner that is similar to the sin of the angels.

How does an angel sin? If an angel is on a specific level, and the angel wants to elevate itself prior to the designated time, the angel is deemed to be a sinner. Likewise, in the Messianic era, if a Jew is on a particular level and wants to elevate themselves prior to the designated time, this will be considered a sin. This is alluded to in this verse:

> And also the priests who go near to the Lord shall prepare themselves, lest the Lord wreak destruction upon them.
> (Shemot 19:22)

---

125. *Ahavat Yehonatan*

We can explain this verse to be alluding to a Jew needing to prepare themselves when attempting to come closer to God and not attempting to do so before the selected time, in the Messianic era.[126]

Mitzvoth

The Talmud (Niddah 61b) brings an opinion that in the Messianic era that all mitzvoth will no longer apply. How are we to understand this opinion?

The law is that if someone was on the spiritual level of Rabbi Shimon bar Yochai, he would not be obligated to observe the mitzvoth. Rabbi Shimon bar Yochai was completely and totally devoted to Torah study. Every waking minute was devoted to the study of Torah. He therefore was exempt from fulfilling the mitzvoth.

In the Messianic era, the Jewish people will have no need to be involved in pursuing a living; they will have no desire for earthly pleasures. Their only desire would be to study God's wisdom. The Jewish people would be on the same level as Rabbi Shimon bar Yochai; they therefore would be exempt from performing the mitzvoth.

In the Messianic era, the mitzvoth will definitely apply; rather, the Jew will not be obligated to fulfill them since they will be completely preoccupied in the study of God's Torah.

---

126. *Ahavat Yehonatan*

Acknowledgments

From Julie and Richie Gerber

Special thanks to Rabbi Efraim Duchman for the introduction to Rabbi Barber.

Thank you so much, Rabbi Yacov Barber, for making our much desired dream into an awe-inspiring reality.

At this very special time in our lives, when we feel connected to our insightful forefather, we also think about members of our family who have passed. We remember José and Josefina Ejbszyc, the patriarch and matriarch of the family; Mrs. Ana Ejbszyc, Julie's mother; and Ana's siblings, Dr. Enrique Eiber, Mrs. Berta Fuchs, and Mr. Julio Ejbszyc. May their memories be for a blessing.

Richie pauses as well and remembers those in his family: Sam and Pearl Gerber, Richie's father and mother. Richie's now passed aunts and uncles—Aunt Molly and Uncle Aron Furman, Uncle Hymie and Aunt Tillie, Uncle Max and Aunt Ruth, Uncle Dave and Aunt Lila, and Uncle Dave and Aunt Henrietta. Richie's brother Edwin Gerber and Cousin Shirley. May Hashem bless them all.

We would like to thank Kim and Al Eiber for their support of this book project.

Thanks to our friends, The Book Couple: Carol Killman Rosenberg and Gary Rosenberg, who exceeded our expectations with editorial and design work on this book.

Appreciations to Sinai Publishers, Tel Aviv, for granting permission to use the image on the cover.

Thanks to Tim Sample for the logo of Gerber's Miracle Publishers.

We lovingly dedicate this book to our son, Isaac Pablo, and his wife, Christine Gerber, and their beautiful son, Toby Simon—the miracles of our life.

Index

Nechemiah, Rabbi. *See* Meir, Rabbi

Nehardea (city), 211

Netanel, Korban, 4

New Year, 241

night time, 9, 222, 239

Noach, 11–14, 34

non-believers, 200, 201

North Pole, 238

Nota, Nosson, 3

numbers

age and, 111

God's name and, 217–218

of Jewish males, 40, 73

of men Korach took to confront
    Moshe, 80–81

of Moshe's prayers to be allowed to
    enter Israel, 94

of officers the Pharaoh took to
    capture Jewish men, 40

spelling of *vov* and, 226–227

value of letters in Hebrew alphabet,
    244

of Ya'akov and family in Egypt,
    244–245

numerous (*rav*), 84

officers (*sholishim*), 40

Oholiab, 53

oil, anointing, 47

Olam HaBa, 151, 183–184

old (*ziknah*), 75

Oppenheim, Dovid, 4

oral tradition. *See* Mishkan (oral
    tradition)

Ovadiah (Prophet), 215

oxen, 102

paschal lamb. *See* lambs: paschal
    (*korban Pesach*)

peace (*shalom*), 181, 208–209, 236

Peor (idol), 104

persecution, 212–214

Pesach, 18, 52, 148, 151, 154–180

Pharaoh, 29, 31, 32, 36–39, 154,
    158–162

belief that children of Jewish people
    born in Egypt were illegitimate,
    87–88, 176

drowning of his men at the Reed
    Sea, 171–174, 178

God's instruction to Moshe on what
    to tell him about Jewish people's
    exile, 158–159

not listening to God, 162

number of men he took with him at
    the exodus, 40

order to cast Jewish boys into sea,
    176

Philistines, 175

Pileshes (nation), 175

Pinchas, 86

Pirkei Avot, 75, 134, 203, 208

plagues, 162–163, 235

planets, 123, 238

pleasures, 65, 243, 246

pogroms, 222

poor, 240

prayers, 61, 107–109, 133, 134, 140,
    165, 203, 232

preacher (*darshan*), 4

present, 28

prophets, 178–179, 206–207

false, 122–123

See also names of individual prophets

prosecutors, 135

Proverbs. *See* Mishlei (Proverbs)

punishment, 11, 13, 64, 157, 162,
    202–203, 206, 239

Purim, 149–150

purity, 87–88, 92, 161, 163, 219,
    233–234

See also impurity

About the Translator

Rabbi Yacov Barber is the child of Holocaust survivors. He is the father of six children and a proud grandfather. He has lived and studied in Israel, Canada, and Melbourne, Australia, and currently resides in New York. Having received both rabbinic ordination and judiciary ordination, he has also completed courses in palliative care, mediation, family violence, and arbitration.

Rabbi Barber is an internationally acclaimed motivational speaker and a much sought-after communicator on ethics and spiritual and personal growth. He has lectured across the United States, Europe, and Canada. He is the author of *Generation to Generation: Insights into the Haggadah* and *Wit & Wisdom: Sermons on the Weekly Torah Reading*. Visit his website at rabbibarber.com.

Made in United States
North Haven, CT
10 June 2024

53437780R10157